COBRA℠

The X Factor in Strategy Execution

Patrick D. Curran

authorHOUSE®

AuthorHouse™
1663 Liberty Drive, Suite 200
Bloomington, IN 47403
www.authorhouse.com
Phone: 1-800-839-8640

First published by AuthorHouse 05/11/2009

ISBN: 978-1-4389-2480-9 (sc)
ISBN: 978-1-4389-2481-6 (hc)

Library of Congress Control Number: 2009902782

Printed in the United States of America
Bloomington, Indiana

This book is printed on acid-free paper.

Dedication:

This book is dedicated to Andrew A. David, 1934-2000. Andrew graduated in Business Studies from Trinity College Dublin in 1957. The same year he joined the Leventis Group in Ghana where ultimately he managed Accra's Coca-Cola Bottling Plant.

In 1963 he moved to Nigeria as Managing Director of Nigerian Bottling Company. He was promoted in 1974 to the Managing Director of Leventis Overseas in London, and acquired Coca-Cola Bottlers in Ireland in 1977 and in Greece in 1981.

In due course the outstanding performance of these operations put the group in a position to take on new Coca-Cola franchises in Eastern Europe under Hellenic Bottling Company (HBC). In 2000 HBC acquired Coca-Cola Beverages and now operates in 28 countries as Coca-Cola Hellenic.

Andrew was an outstanding executive and an extraordinary entrepreneur. He absolutely loved the Coca-Cola business. He had a rare talent for spotting business opportunities, and was fearless in exploiting them. Andrew's vision, values and work practices shaped HBC's culture...a culture driven by operational excellence and customer satisfaction.

Table of Contents

Forward ***xi***

Part 1: The 3 Points of Pressure

Chapter 1 COBRA: The X Factor in Strategy Execution ***3***
COBRA is a process for aligning the organization with a changing environment so that strategy can be executed. It is the X factor in strategy execution that provides a unique advantage that cannot be easily replicated by its competitors.

Chapter 2 Globalization and the Transformation of Business ***5***
In practically every case, the inability of the organization to execute the strategy is linked to one or more of three factors: the structure, the system or the culture. COBRA provides change interventions to realign these Three Points of Pressure.

Chapter 3 Aligning the Culture ***19***
Culture is the human side of the organization, the beliefs, the values, and the work practices. Four indispensable components of a well aligned culture are: Leadership, Vision & Values, Norms, and Core Competencies. Assessment tools and change interventions for each are discussed.

Chapter 4 Aligning the Structure ***35***
The structure of an organization is the formal arrangement of functions, levels, and processes, as well as the roles

and responsibilities for working within and across these arrangements. Four components of a well aligned structure will be discussed: the formal structure, boundary management, core business processes, and bridging structures. Assessment tools and change interventions for each are discussed.

The best performance management systems have five components working together like the fingers of a hand. They are simple in design and disciplined in execution. Examples of the five components and the five attributes of the system are discussed.

Part 2: Designing the Performance Management System

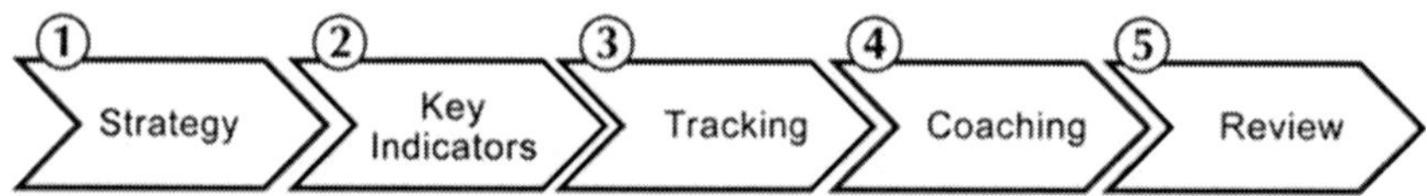

The system is the great flywheel of execution. We will examine the five components one by one in separate chapters, including best practices and structured processes for aligning each.

Strategic planning identifies the best competitive fit for a company based on its strengths and the opportunities that exist or emerge in the business environment. The COBRA Alignment Process that guides the development of both strategic and organizational plans is discussed.

Key indicators translate strategic plans into measurable performance. Best practices, three types of key indicators, and a process for identifying them are discussed.

Effective performance tracking involves gathering, processing and transmitting information to the user in a timely, accurate

Forward

Although Pat Curran and I had been colleagues in The Coca-Cola Company during the 1979's it was not until 1983 that our paths first crossed, when as CEO of Coca-Cola HBC in Greece I asked Pat---who had moved into management consultancy—for assistance. Little did either of us realize back then that our initial meeting would lead to a quarter of a century of a wonderful friendship during which Pat developed and constantly refined the system he christened COBRA.

In the early 1980's our organizational needs in CCHBC were pretty basic. We were moving from an organization that had been structured along traditional functional lines to a decentralized profit-center basis. We were fortunate to have many capable managers willing to embrace change provided they were convinced that the position of CEO was stable. During the previous thirteen years they had worked for eight different CEOs. Initially we desired nothing more than better communication and teamwork, to have less protection of individual kingdoms and to have better dialogue between various functions, so that the total company benefitted.

As the '80s unfolded, we launched Amita, our own brand of juices, and started to expand into the Balkans and Russia thanks to a vote of confidence from The Coca-Cola Company. Eventually this growth made CCHBC the 3rd largest bottler in the Coca-Cola Global family.

The expansion required that we standardize the performance management system across the group while allowing for national and cultural differences. We were confident that we had the know-how and the product portfolio to be successful; the challenge was in building an organization to make it happen. The management system required a common strategic planning process based on the needs of the overall group as well as the needs of the many local markets. We also had to agree on common performance indicators and tracking systems across the group while providing for flexibility at the local level.

Many of the scale economies of expanding the group came from pool purchasing and the consolidation of manufacturing operations. This however entailed a significant increase in the movement of raw materials, sales assets, and finished goods across the organization, which required extraordinary planning and coordination. Processes had to be streamlined, and boundaries had to be managed. Finally, we wanted to create a shared culture based on the core values of teamwork, operational excellence and customer satisfaction, while building on the strengths of the local cultures.

COBRA provided us with a standard way to realign the structure, the system, and the culture throughout the group, while allowing for the input and participation of each country. Market execution had always been a core competency of CCHBC. COBRA enabled us to build on that strength during a period of rapid expansion.

COBRA succeeds when top management is committed and a 'COBRA manager' is appointed to support business unit managers in the initial phase of implementation. If top management only pays lip service results will almost definitely disappoint.

I heartily recommend COBRA as developed by Pat Curran and described in the following pages as valuable reading for any CEO or senior manager who is looking for ideas which work in solving communication and alignment issues in his/her organization.

Gerard A. Reidy
Former CEO, Coca-Cola HBC,
1981-1995

Part 1: The 3 Points of Pressure

Chapters 1-5 explain how to align the organization with the business environment so that strategy can be executed. Interventions for aligning the Three Points of Pressure—the culture, the structure, and the system--are discussed.

Chapter 1
COBRA: The X Factor in Strategy Execution

Companies that prosper in turbulent times are strategically agile in identifying opportunities, and organizationally agile in exploiting them. Getting the strategy right is more important than ever. Yet it is not enough, if it can't be executed.

This book is based on the premise that execution matters as much or more than strategy in a global environment. As Larry Bossidy and Ram Charan have noted:

> ***"Execution is the great unaddressed issue in the world today. Its absence is the single biggest obstacle to success and the cause of most of the disappointments that are mistakenly attributed to other causes."*** [1]

What then explains execution breakdowns in spite of sound strategy? The answer is a lack of alignment between the strategy and the organization. In practically every case, the failure is linked to one or more of three factors:

- The organization's structure is flawed
- The management system doesn't support the strategy
- The culture gets in the way

Realigning the strategy can take days or weeks, while realigning the organization can take months or years. If you fall behind --if the organization is not ready to execute the strategy -- you may not catch up. It is no longer good enough to fix the organization this year based on last year's execution breakdowns. If the strategy can change in a heartbeat, then the organization must be ready to execute the strategy in a heartbeat.

Here's the good news. Realigning the organization need not be an epic, "bet the farm" ordeal. COBRA is an early warning and response system that keeps the organization aligned with the realities of the business environment. It is the X factor in strategy execution that is not easily replicated by your competitors.

Why the name COBRA? It is an acronym for:

Crossing Organization Boundaries Reinforcing Alignments

In this book the term "boundary" means membrane like the kind that surrounds a living cell. In business, a healthy boundary provides internal integrity while facilitating the flow of information, expertise and energy. A disruptive boundary impedes the flow.

Alignment cannot occur in an organization segmented by disruptive boundaries. Execution suffers and strategy fails. We will have more to say about boundaries in the next chapter.

The concepts and tools discussed in this book are based on over 20 years of experience with US and multi-national clients.

****

The name COBRA calls to mind one of nature's most amazing creatures. The Cobra is unique among snakes in that it can quickly change its shape. When threatened or disturbed, it raises the front part of its body and flattens it neck to display its hood. This transformation is known to stop elephants in their tracks. The Cobra executes with agility. It is fearless. Just as companies shaped by COBRA are agile and fearless.

Chapter 2
Globalization and the Transformation of Business

What in the world happened?

For some companies the last quarter of the 20th century has been a golden age of growth and prosperity; for others it has been the end of the road.

The sweep of change has been stunning - the fall of the Iron Curtain; the worldwide web; the economic emergence of China and India are just a few examples of rapid change that has brought both extraordinary problems and extraordinary opportunities.

For decades after World War II, America was an economic juggernaut fueled by a large market, technological superiority, a skilled workforce and an abundance of investment capital. Productivity grew steadily from 1948 to 1973. In this relatively stable period most US companies could establish and execute their strategy in a "steady state" organization. Change happened, but the pace was deliberate enough to allow for incremental adjustment.

Then came the 1980s, and things started to unravel. America began to lose its competitive edge to other economies. "Growth of productivity has been slower in the past 15 years (1972-1987) than it was for at least two decades before" observed The MIT Commission on Industrial Productivity, "Moreover, the rate of productivity improvement in the United States has fallen behind that in several Western European and Asian nations." [1] Globalization was no longer a fascinating abstraction. It was a threatening fact.

The world's consuming population – participants in the global economy – grew from 2.5 billion in 1985 to over 6 billion in 2007. In that 22 year span, the heavy concentration of consumers in North America, Western Europe and Japan gave way to a worldwide distribution that touched nearly every nation in the world. This larger, more diverse, and more dispersed consumer population turned traditional business models on their head.

Snapshot of Change through Globalization: Consumers and Beverages

The speed and magnitude of change in the beverage business, an industry in which our firm has worked extensively for years, has been extraordinary. This change is typical of the impact that globalization has had on all industries. So let's take a look.

- ***Changing Consumer Needs and Wants*** - from traditional carbonated soft drinks to water, juices, health drinks, sports drinks, energy drinks, and more.

- ***Growth in Package and Product Portfolio*** - the shift in consumer needs triggered dramatic growth in new products and packages. Most major bottlers grew from 40 or 50 SKUs (stock keeping units) to over 300.

- ***Speed to Market*** - responding to changing consumer needs with a vastly expanded product portfolio requires speed to market as well as superior execution at the point of purchase. The need for speed in gaining trial and repeat purchase of an expanding array of products puts great demands on the total system. Like fly fishing, you need to select the right fly, but presentation is what catches fish.

- ***Consolidation of the Retail Trade*** - there has been an intensifying concentration of retailers in the last 20 years. A few giants like Wal-Mart, Tescos, and Carrefour now predominate. Convenience stores and fast-food restaurants have followed the same trend. Fewer, larger retail customers have more buying power and more influence over suppliers than did individual players in the fragmented retail market of the past.

- ***Consolidation of Bottling Franchises*** – to achieve the scale economies needed to survive in a highly competitive market and to better serve their larger customers, bottlers needed to consolidate. In the 1970s, the US had approximately 370 independent Coca-Cola franchise bottlers, most being third generation family-owned businesses. Today a single franchise, Coca-Cola Enterprises (CCE), sells approximately 80 percent of The Coca-Cola Company's bottle and can volume in North America. As further evidence of growth through globalization, CCE also operates in Canada, Belgium, continental France, Great Britain, Luxembourg, Monaco and the Netherlands.

Welcome to the global economy, where nothing is like it used to be – or will be tomorrow.

When Worlds Collide

Our consulting engagements in the beverage industry over the last twenty years have given us a firsthand view of how globalization impacts the traditional organization. Let's consider just one example. As mentioned above, in the past most major bottlers produced and marketed approximately 50 SKUs, taking into account the varieties of brands, flavors and packages. Analyzing what it takes to get one SKU to market, there are on average 20 boundary transactions. They start with procurement and extend all the way to placing the finished product on the store shelf.

At 50 SKUs with 20 transactions for each, the business of yesteryear needed to make a total of around 1000 hand-offs for all its products. Think of each hand-off as a "boundary crossing" that occurs between different levels and functions of the company.

The same company today is dealing with 300 SKUs, because it is targeting a much broader consumer base with a huge diversity of preferences and tastes. This means the company now must manage 6000 boundary crossings.

Feeling the Stress

Not surprisingly, this six fold increase in boundary activity has put a tremendous stress on the bottler's ability to execute strategy. It has had a domino effect across the organization that has impacted many functions and processes: procurement, new product development, supply chain, sales forecasting, production planning, manufacturing, and market execution. And the growth in SKUs is but one of many demands put on the traditional organization.

As usual, Peter Drucker saw this coming. He predicted the collision of the traditional organization and globalization as early as 1983.

"The next twenty-five years will be the adolescent crisis of management." [2]

All industries have experienced this "adolescent crisis of management" on a significant scale. In more stable times, managers could --plan their work and then work their plan --with the existing organization. When change did happen, it required incremental adjustments: tweaking the strategy, moving the boxes around on the org chart, or extending the life cycle of a product in decline. Now, a profound and comprehensive transformation is required.

This transformation is far more than the "what-if" scenarios and the "if-then" contingencies that are built into the business plan. Those tend to focus on change as exceptional events rather than on change as a constant condition.

Drucker also observed that managers who learned their craft in more stable times had little experience in implementing change in turbulent times. In the past the need to do so was rare. For the same reason, there were few credible tools at hand to assess the alignment of the organization, or to expedite the realignment process.

In Search of Silver Bullets

Recognizing that rapid adaptation to change was not one of their strengths, companies looked to the experts to come in and show them how. An onslaught of ready-made solutions poured forth from business schools and consulting firms. They included: Zero-Based Budgeting, Benchmarking, Reengineering, Total Quality Management, Six Sigma, Participative Management, Competency-Based Development, Rightsizing, and so on. Some were shamelessly promoted in the business media as paradigm-shifting, quantum-leaping, all-purpose cure-alls. The trouble was, few companies had the skill to diagnose what they really needed or to choose a program on that basis. The search was on for a silver bullet.

Chart 1 illustrates the programs that came (and often went) between 1950 and the turn of the century.[3] The vertical axis shows the frequency with which each of these programs was mentioned in *The New York Times*, *the Wall Street Journal*, and the *Reader's Guide to Periodical Literature.*

Chart 1

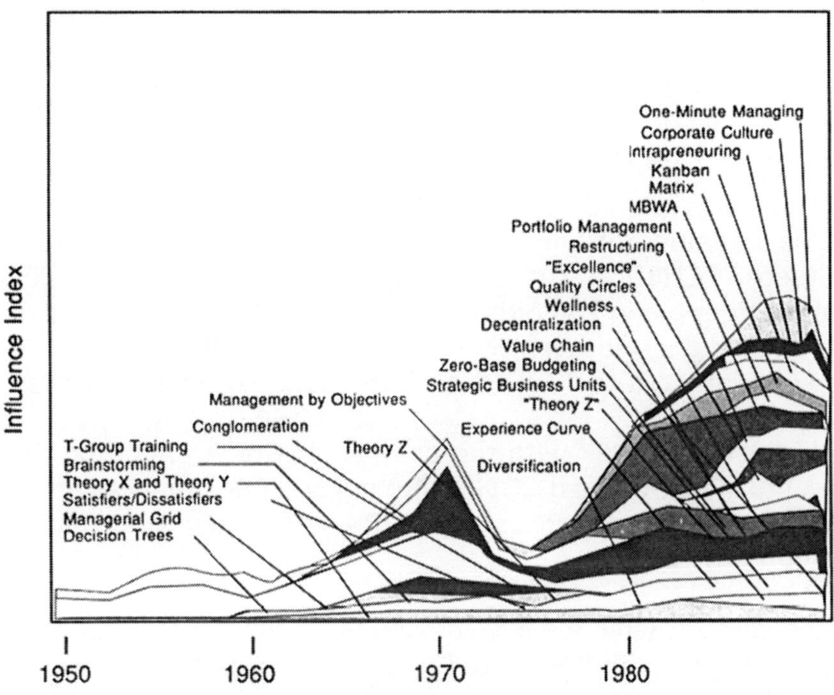

Think of this chart as a visualization of Drucker's "adolescent crisis of management," with worried companies frantically searching here and there to unlock the mysteries of executing well in the midst of accelerating change. Some companies survived this crisis, some did not, and some are still working their way through the process as you read these pages.

While a few of these programs, like Corporate Culture, have taken hold and stayed around. Most failed to address fundamental alignment problems and are hardly remembered today. In their time, however, they exacted an enormous human and economic cost. They turned organizations upside down while creating false expectations.

Our firm, along with our clients, did plenty of trial and error learning during this time. We, too, fell in and out of love with various programs. Along the way, we came to realize that the whole matter was a good bit simpler than the silver-bullet programs would have people think--simpler, but not easier.

What companies need is the ability to align their organization with a changing environment so strategy can be well executed. This is what COBRA does.

Looking Deeper

COBRA was piloted with one of our long-time clients, the Coca-Cola Hellenic Bottling Company (CCHBC). Based in Athens, Greece, CCHBC is a going concern. It currently serves 550 million people in 28 countries, and has achieved double-digit growth in the last seven years. Its product portfolio consists of 147 carbonated soft drinks and 461 non-carbonated drinks.

We started in 1987 with the company's Greek operation and eventually introduced COBRA into many of the other countries. Meanwhile, we began using COBRA with many other clients around the world.

Two decades later, we have developed a substantial data base reflecting the conditions we find in companies at the start of a COBRA engagement. These projects generally kickoff with an organizational assessment called COBRA-Scan, which entails direct observation of work practices, interviews with internal and final customers, and a readiness survey. All levels and functions are included in the scan.

What we have found is a surprising consistency about disruptive boundaries in spite of differences among the companies at the time they engaged us. Some had been very successful in the past but were no longer growing. Some were greenfield start-ups. Some were recent acquisitions in both mature and developing markets. Though most of these companies had a significant market share, they were all struggling to execute in a turbulent business environment.

Consider these consolidated survey findings from our clients in thirteen countries on four continents. There were many positive findings to be sure; these, however, were the most common problems we found:

- Employees consistently rate the functional performance management system of the company much higher (8.2) on a ten point scale than its cross-functional performance management system (4.8).

- When asked about improving the formal structure of the organization, more than half offer suggestions that translate into reducing the disruptive boundaries between functions and levels.

- We also ask a culturally related question - when conflict occurs between departments, do employees do what is best for themselves, their department or the organization as a whole? Only 25% think their colleagues would do what's best for the organization.

In open-ended questions, we asked survey respondents to describe the types of disruptive boundaries they experienced. Here's what they told us.

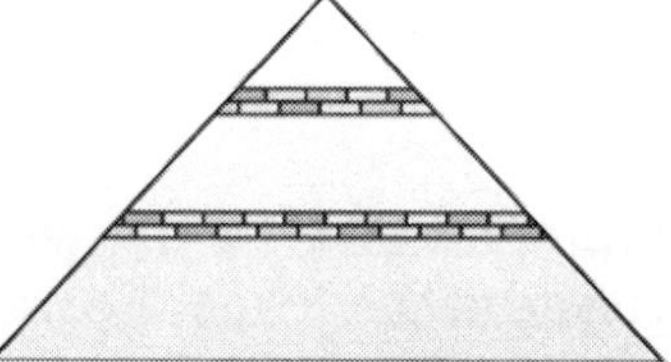

Between Levels:

- Too many levels, too many boundaries to cross

- Strategic plans "parked" at the head office rather than in the field
- Key indicators, information systems and reviews not well aligned across levels
- Not enough autonomy at lower levels to exploit local market opportunities
- A culture that discourages open communication between levels
- Responsibility for planning and execution are separated

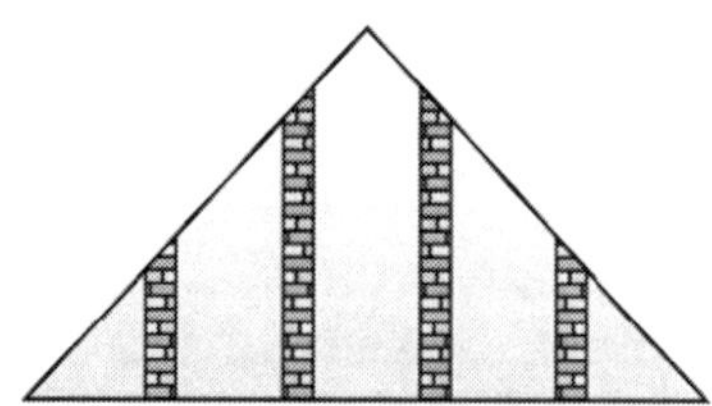

***Across Functions*:**

- The absence of common values to foster teamwork throughout the organization
- Competing functional objectives—not aligned in the planning process
- Absence of roles and responsibilities for cross-functional work
- Key indicators overly focused on functional performance
- Little accountability for internal or final customer satisfaction
- Contentious sub-cultures discourage collaboration

Again and again we found a similar pattern --disruptive boundaries form --when the structure, the system, and the culture are not aligned across levels and functions. Disruptive boundaries don't allow information, energy and expertise to flow back and forth inside the organization, or with customers or other external stakeholders. Execution suffers and strategy fails.

In the development of COBRA, we expected boundaries to surface as an issue in the scans. We were surprised, however, that they were so pervasive. In their landmark study *Organizations and Environment*, Paul Lawrence and Jay Lorsh observed that as organizations become larger, they differentiate into parts, and the management of these parts has to be integrated to operate effectively.[4] Rosabeth Moss Kanter in her study of innovative companies found that a segmented structure stifles innovation.

"The primary set of roadblocks to innovation result from segmentation: a structure finely divided into departments and levels, each with a tall fence around it and communication in and out restricted - indeed, carefully guarded...the sheer height of hierarchy contributed to a second common characteristic of less innovating companies: the virtual absence of lateral cooperation or communication and support across areas." [5]

The negative correlation between a segmented structure and innovation has huge implications for a 21st Century Company. The global consumer demands the newest, the best quality, and the best value. Meeting these demands calls for an organization that is smarter, faster, and more agile than competition. Traditional organizations, with their tendency to segment, cannot deliver. Something new is needed.

Development of COBRA--Testing the Concept

Earlier I acknowledged that our firm experimented with some of the silver-bullet models. We found most were inappropriate or insufficient. Based on our research and first-hand experience, we were confident that the structure, system, and culture played a major role in the alignment process. We suspected, however, that there was more to it than that.

Toward this end, we analyzed various organizational design models. Each identified a number of key success factors that contributed to an organization's effectiveness. Chart 2 illustrates a model with six factors that need to be aligned in order to reduce disruptive boundaries and optimize execution.

Chart 2

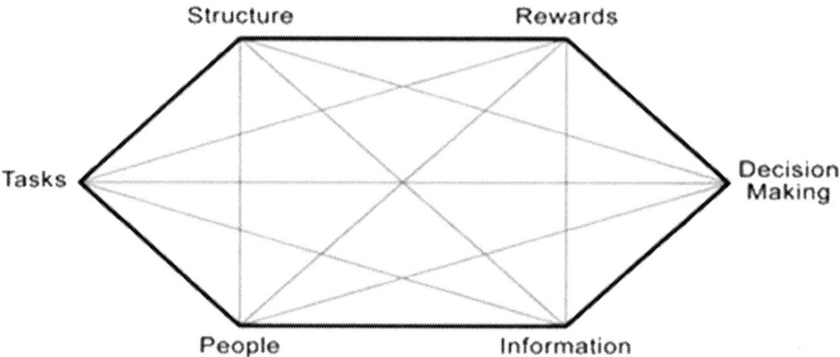

Additional factors were identified in other models: staff, identity, technology, key relationships, and the dominant coalition. All of these factors certainly have a role to play in building a high-performance organization. We are particularly indebted to John Kotter[6], Richard Pascale[7], and David Hanna.[8] Three of the models we studied were developed by these management scholars. Over the years we gathered data on fifteen of these factors and analyzed the extent to which they created or reduced disruptive boundaries.

As it turned out, our findings confirmed our initial assumptions. With client after client, 80% of the disruptive boundaries we encountered were caused by only 20% of the likely causes --the structure, the system and the culture. We learned that the pressure for change, the pressure to open disruptive boundaries, had to be focused on these three factors, which we call the *Three Points of Pressure.* Align these factors, and the rest will follow.

Thereafter, the *Three Points of Pressure* became the "vital signs" we focused on in diagnosing the wellness of an organization, and prescribing a cure if needed.

The Three Points of Pressure--Applying the Concept

Next, we experimented with various methods to assess the alignment of the structure, the system and the culture. This led to the development of the COBRA-Scan assessment tool--more about that later. Finally we experimented with various change interventions for realigning the organization. Here again, we learned a lot along the way:

- Many of the silver-bullet programs designed to increase productivity and cut costs served only as cosmetic-overlays on dysfunctional organizations. They created a parallel structure. Managers were asked to demonstrate progress with the program, while getting their real work done with the existing organization. Not good. These programs certainly have their place when built on a firm foundation—an aligned culture, structure and system.[9]

- A well designed change of the formal structure that doesn't explicitly define the roles and responsibilities required to manage across organizational boundaries will have little impact on performance. Both human and technical factors need to be considered in making changes to the structure.

- A culture intervention calling for changes in core values and attitudes, that isn't linked to changes in management practices and performance measures, will have little impact on performance. Culture change needs to be aligned with the management system.

- A change intervention that involves a company-wide training program designed to change individual managers is less effective than an intervention that directly changes the system, structure, and culture in a specific business unit--since the current system is more likely to change the individual than the individual is to change the system.[10]

The COBRA alignment process was developed from these learnings.

Crossing **O**rganizational **B**oundaries **R**einforcing **A**lignments

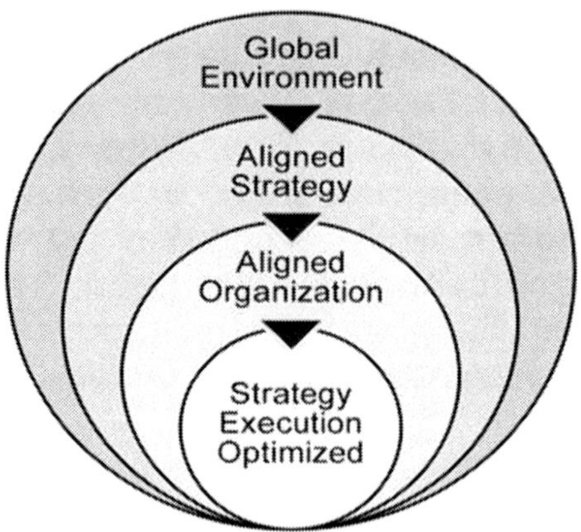

In summary, to prosper in a global environment, you need a strategy that exploits current and emerging opportunities (an aligned strategy) and an organization that can execute the strategy (an aligned organization).

An aligned organization is not fragmented by disruptive boundaries. It is aligned vertically from top to bottom, and horizontally across functions to the final customer. These reinforcing alignments create a balance of performance pressure that drives excellence in both functional and cross-functional work. Aligned organizations are characterized by speed, agility and self-correction. They can absorb change and respond quickly.

And finally we learned that the *Three Points of Pressure* are the key factors in keeping the organization aligned. They are the points where the pressure needs to be applied--continuously monitoring the current alignment and implementing the needed changes. This can be summarized in the following way: a company's execution capability, its ExCap, is a function of the leader's skill (L) in aligning the structure, the system and the culture.

ExCap = L x (Structure + System + Culture)

These are 21st Century survival skills, and they are needed by business leaders at every level of the organization. To change the metaphor, think of the *Three Points of Pressure* as the load-bearing beams of the organization. They create the platform that everything else runs on. If they are not aligned, all the other programs, processes, and change interventions will have a limited impact. Any effort to improve the effectiveness of the organization should start with the alignment of these three factors.

These then are the basic principles of the COBRA alignment process that will be discussed in the remaining chapters of this book.

COBRA in Action

As described earlier, COBRA-Scan is the starting point. It assesses the *Three Points of Pressure* and the key drivers that underpin each, as illustrated in chart 3 below. The scan provides a more comprehensive and accurate assessment of the organization than can be achieved with traditional assessment tools such as SWOT or Force Field Analysis.

Chart 3

Three Points of Pressure		
Structure	System	Culture
Formal Structure	*Strategy*	*Leadership*
Boundary Mgmt.	*Key Indicators*	*Vision & Values*
Core Processes	*Tracking Systems*	*Norms*
Bridging Structures	*On-Job Coaching*	*Core Competencies*
	Review	

In the next chapter, we will provide interventions to realign the culture. Chapter 4 will provide interventions to realign the structure. And chapters 5-10 will provide interventions to realign the performance management system.

Chapter Summary

COBRA is the X factor in strategy execution. Leaders that master the alignment process can execute their strategy today, and stay ahead of the curve in executing their strategy in the future. They have the capacity to effect renewal and sustain growth.

Chapter 3
Aligning the Culture

Culture can foster passion and purpose or conflict and entitlement.

Culture deals with the human side of the organization: the beliefs, the values, and the competencies of the people. It is the first of the *Three Points of Pressure* that we will explore in depth.

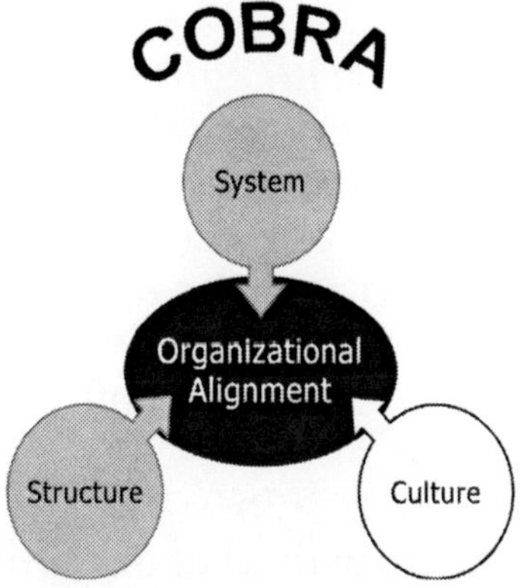

One common definition of culture is "*the way we do things around here to succeed.*" [1] But as we shall see, culture often gets in the way of success.

How is culture formed? Think of it as part chicken and part egg. Culture is shaped by the environment and the values of the founders. Yet once embedded in the collective DNA of the organization, it shapes the values and behavior of those who follow.

When aligned with strategy, culture is a major asset that fosters purpose, passion and excellence. When misaligned it becomes a significant liability, breeding conflict, bureaucracy and a sense of entitlement.

In this chapter we will investigate three cultural continuums, and discuss ways to build an enabling culture. But first, let's look at how culture became such an important business concept. It wasn't always so.

Recognition of Culture as a Business Factor

Not much was made of corporate culture before the 80's. Today no one disputes its pivotal role in determining how well organizations perform. John Kotter and James Heskett investigated the cultures of 207 organizations between 1987 and 1991 to understand the connection between culture and economic performance. What they learned intensified the focus on culture as a high-impact factor.

"We found that firms with cultures that emphasized all the key managerial constituencies (customer, stockholders, and employees) and leadership from managers at all levels out performed firms that did not have those cultural traits by a huge margin." [2]

Later research by James C. Collins and Jerry I.Porras further reinforced these findings.[3]

These studies matched up with what our firm was experiencing with our clients. In working with numerous franchise bottling operations that had similar systems and structures, the importance of culture stood out. Those that focused on operational excellence (hands-on-detail-driven) and promoted the values of teamwork and customer service were significantly more successful than the rest.

Not surprisingly, culture is highly interdependent with the other two points of pressure. It can influence the way the system and structure operate, and the system and structure can affect the culture by either creating silos or promoting synergy. The MIT Commission on Industrial Productivity had this to say on the subject.

"Many companies have stated their intention to reduce the number of layers in their organization

hierarchy and achieve greater cross-functional integration but have difficulty putting their ideas into practice. Successful implementation typically requires a change in company culture that encourages and supports participation, teamwork, and decision making at lower levels of the organization." [4]

****

Three Cultural Continuums

Three types of cultural continuums are discussed below. The preferred culture for each generally lies mid-way between the extremes. In order to "unfreeze" and realign a dysfunctional culture, the pendulum often needs to swing beyond the mid-point in the other direction.

Strategic-Operational

Some organizations are very good at adapting strategy to changes in the business environment, but they lack the operational savvy to execute effectively. Other companies are excellent operators. They are able to deliver both productivity and customer satisfaction in the here and now, but are less competent in detecting shifts in the market and reacting in appropriate ways. The best companies are balanced-- both strategically agile and operationally disciplined.

Entitlement-Fear

Dr. Judith Bardwick in her book *Danger in the Comfort Zone* describes how performance pressure or stress can shape culture.[5] Companies that exert too much performance pressure risk creating a culture of fear. People become frozen, unwilling to initiate or to take risks. Conversely companies that exert too little performance pressure can create a culture of entitlement. This manifests itself in an attitude of "you owe me--my needs are more important than the needs of the company or the customer." Companies that tilt toward entitlement become internally focused and operationally flabby. Often a company that has experienced years of growth and prosperity becomes complacent, as occurred in the American auto industry in the '80s. Again, the best companies are balanced. They exert performance pressure along with supportive coaching – an equilibrium of heat and light.

Exploiting-Exploring

The third continuum comes from the work of James March.[6] "Exploitation refers to ... short-term improvement, refinement, routinization and elaboration ... it thrives on focused attention, precision, repetition, analysis, sanity, discipline and control." Conversely, "exploration refers to experimentation ... in hopes of finding alternatives that improve on old ones. It thrives on serendipity risk taking, novelty, free association, madness, loose discipline, and relaxed control." The explorers create new products; the exploiters capitalize on them. It takes a balance of exploration and exploitation to optimize performance.

Considering how many places a company might fall along each of the three continuums, it is clear that there are many gradations of culture. The challenge for leaders is to create a culture that fits the company, based on the task requirements, the industry, and the competitive environment.

2. Building an Enabling Culture

Of the *Three Points of Pressure*, culture is the most elusive and intangible. Think of an alpine peak. Sometimes the summit is visible, and sometimes clouds get in the way--while the base is clear. Culture is like that.

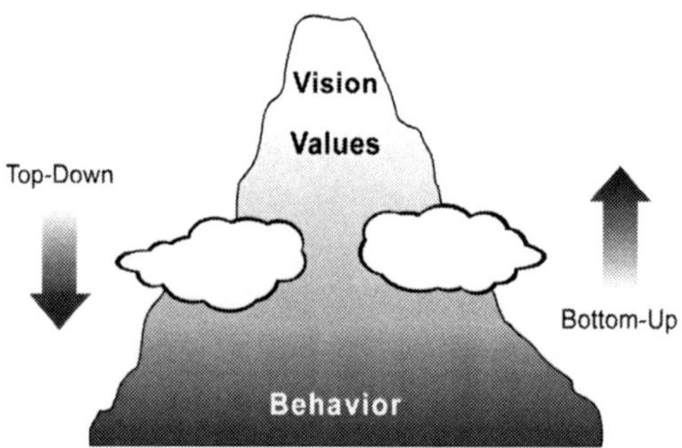

At the summit we find the company's vision - which defines its purpose and destination - and its values - which articulate core beliefs such as integrity, teamwork and customer service.

Vision and values need to come from the top. It takes time for them to take hold in a company, so that acting upon them becomes second nature.

At the base of the mountain--there for all to see--are the behaviors of the organization--those concrete actions that cause vision and values to come alive. Behaviors are more tangible and easier to change. Making collaborative decisions, responding to customer complaints, giving positive feedback are examples of observable behaviors.

Culture takes its strength from the summit and from the base of the mountain. When vision and values are deeply felt, clearly articulated and modeled by the leadership team, then culture is built from the top, and cascades down to every level. And yes, sometimes clouds get in the way. When vision and values are proclaimed from the top, but not practiced, they become a sham. Contentious sub-cultures that segment the company often fill the gap.

Culture is also built from the bottom-up when specific behaviors, norms, and work practices that consistently deliver results are encouraged and supported. A combination of top-down and bottom-up culture-building is the best way to create an enabling culture. All levels of management have a role to play.

Remember, there are many synergies among the *3 Points of Pressure*. Aligning the structure and system with the strategy (to be discussed in later chapters) will develop roles, work practices and norms that become rooted in the culture. It all works together.

Our firm uses COBRA-Scan to evaluate how well the culture supports the strategy. We gather data through interviews, an organizational readiness survey, 360° feedback, and on-job observation. There are four indispensable elements to a culture that support strategy execution:

Culture: Keys to Execution

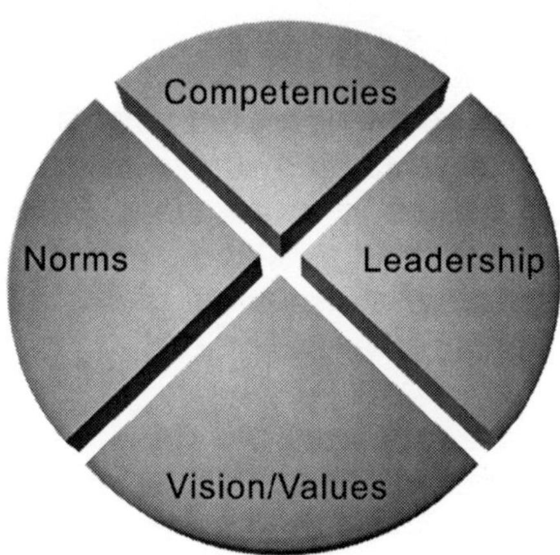

Leadership

It is difficult to overstate the importance of leadership in building a strong organization and a strong culture. It should be the first item you consider in assessing the alignment of the existing culture. Jim Collins, the best-selling author of *Good to Great,* has this to say about moving good organizations to greatness.

"We expected that good-to-great leaders would begin by setting a new vision and strategy. We found instead that they first got the right people on the bus, the wrong people off the bus, and the right people in the right seats—and then they figured out where to drive it." [7]

Effective leadership is needed at every level, and encompasses many things: the courage to confront the status quo; the humility to admit you are wrong; the candor to deal openly with conflict.

Nowhere is leadership more critical than in building an organization that can execute the strategy. As discussed in chapter 2, a company's execution capability, its (ExCap), is a function of the leader's skill (L) in aligning the structure, the system and the culture.

ExCap = L x (Structure + System + Culture)

Now let's focus on the competencies and character traits that leaders need in order to realign the culture:

- *Cultural Awareness* - Change leaders recognize when the culture is not aligned. They articulate a vision and values to move the company forward. They preserve values and competencies that remain relevant, while changing those that are not.

- *Fit* – Whether the change leader comes from inside or outside, his/her values and beliefs are congruent with the company's values and beliefs. Even great companies like Hewlett-Packard, Delta Air Lines, and The Home Depot have had CEOs who didn't fit the culture. And the results showed it.

- *Courage* - The change leader has the courage to articulate a vision and values that form the cornerstone of their beliefs, and the collaborative skills to overcome political resistance.

Strong leaders can be cultivated – and this happens in an enabling culture. It requires a systematic approach to selection, development and succession planning. We have found peer-based feedback, or 360° feedback, to be a highly effective leadership development tool. It provides confidential feedback to leaders at every level on how satisfied their co-workers are with their day-to-day leadership practices and the way they live the values.

Chart 2 identifies the ten lowest ranked items in a survey composed of 72 items. The managers in this company did many things well. These items, however, are those with the lowest co-worker satisfaction.

Chart 2

Bottom 10 Report / 360° Feedback
1. Has a system to measure internal / external customer satisfaction.
2. Prepares a written development plan for every direct report.
3. Makes people feel like winners.
4. Is willing to challenge higher level management when appropriate.
5. Meets regularly with customers to determine if they are satisfied with our services.
6. Avoids over-controlling the team.
7. Conducts effective review meeting to improve productivity.
8. Coaches their subordinates.
9. Gives regular performance feedback.
10. Takes risks in letting others make decisions.

Notice the pattern. Items 1, 4, and 5 relate to leading across boundaries. The other 7 items reflect leadership skills needed to operate an effective performance management system: providing feedback, coaching, problem solving, and reviewing performance.

Over the years our firm has been involved in thousands of feedback sessions with various clients in many different countries. The above report is very typical regardless of the company or the culture. Leaders at all levels need training and coaching to master these most challenging competencies.

Vision

A vision statement defines a company's purpose and destination. It can be as high-minded as finding a cure for cancer, or as mundane--yet none the less important--as providing the best customer service in the aluminum siding business. The development of the Toyota Prius, the first commercially available hybrid car, provides a good example of the critical role that vision plays in a company's success.[8]

The Toyota Way

One of the core principles of the Toyota Way is to base management decisions on a long term philosophy, even at the expense of short-term goals. The Toyota Way is focused on generating value for the customer, society, and the company.

In 1993, Toyota Chairman Eiji Toyoda set forth a challenging vision-- to develop a method of designing cars for the 21st century. The initial concept was to minimize vehicle size, maximize interior space, and improve fuel economy. Most cars coming out of Detroit at that time were large, polluting, gas guzzlers. After months of losing their way in technical hardware strategies, the Toyota development team finally returned to the Chairman's vision. A 21st century car designed to generate value to customers and society, needed to focus on fuel economy and the environment. The vision and the core principles guided all subsequent development.

In October of 1997 Toyota launched the Prius with its innovative hybrid engine. Its fuel economy was twice that of conventional cars of the same class and it emitted half as much CO^2. It has been an extraordinary technological and environmental breakthrough that did indeed generate value to the customers, society and the company. The strategic plan for developing the Prius could easily have gotten bogged down in technical details without the guidance of the core principles and the Chairman's vision.

Both strategy and vision provide direction, but not the same kind. The vision is a company's definition of success, like a 21st century car designed to generate value to customers and society. The strategy is the game plan for getting there - minimum vehicle size, improved fuel economy, and reduced CO^2 emissions.

Here's another way to think of the difference...the vision is a long-term destination, less influenced by changes in the environment. It helps unify all levels and functions in a common cause. The strategy, with its goals and objectives, is subordinate to the vision, subject to change as needed to achieve the vision.

Values

Values define how we work together, what is okay and what is not okay. The following values are common to many of our clients as well as other companies: integrity, customer service, quality, innovation, teamwork, and shareholder value.

Companies that espouse these values are generally saying one of two things. First, these are current strengths and need to be perpetuated. Alternatively, these are current weaknesses, reflecting a lack of integrity or the absence of teamwork that are preventing us from being successful. And we need to get them right.

In realigning an ineffective culture, it is important to hold on to your strengths as you eliminate your weaknesses. We have worked with companies whose cultures are internally focused and risk-averse, yet also emphasize continuous improvement, effective cost controls, and fair and equitable treatment of people. Once you understand your strengths and weakness, you can identify what needs to change.

For example, ineffective cultures are often not good at adapting to change. The values of innovation, continuous improvement and customer service are particularly important in creating an adaptive culture. A culture that values customer service stays in touch with the changing needs of customers. A culture that values innovation understands that change is constant, and initiates plans and programs to foster innovation.

In turbulent times values trump rules. In an ever-changing environment, it is impossible to anticipate every conceivable situation and create rules and procedures to deal with them all. Work is less programmable, more individual discretion is needed. Values work differently than rules. Values like integrity, customer service, and teamwork define core principles and beliefs. It is left to the individual to determine how these values should be applied depending on the situation.

When values are articulated, modeled and rewarded, they become embedded in the culture and influence behavior as a matter of course. When consequences are not linked to living the values, they can become little more than a public relations exercise.

The Ring of Fire

On paper things looked good. The Moscow operation was a recent acquisition. It served a population of ten million people in the Moscow area—a new plant, a new general manager (GM), a new system. Core values had been articulated and posted on every bulletin board, with customer service and teamwork being critical. Cross-functional roles and responsibilities had been hammered out and agreed to. Everyone understood the values, but when push came to shove people retreated into the safety of their silos.

The new expatriate GM adopted a go-slow approach...'let's get to know the team, let's try to understand the culture, let's create openness and collaboration.' This as it turned out was perceived as weakness.

As summer peak season rolled around, unresolved conflicts between functions were crippling the operation. Out of frustration the GM became more involved, coaching and recommending solutions. Even this was ineffective. The pendulum had swung too far off center—unintentionally he had created an entitled culture. An unfreezing event was called for.

That afternoon when the public address requested that all function heads join the GM in his office, it was not for caviar and vodka. The ensuing discussion could be heard throughout the plant without the aid of the public address system. This became known as the ring of fire. Once consequences, both positive and negative, were linked to the values, the behavior quickly changed.

Managing in a diverse, multicultural environment is a reality in a global market. With the best of intentions, the GM had initially under-led his team. For some, the GM's resolution may seem too strong. Within this cultural context, it was appropriate. The team was skeptical of high-minded values. Once consequences were linked to the values, their behavior quickly changed.

Vision and values are potent tools, but you can't fake them. If the leadership group isn't totally on board in words and actions, the lack of commitment will quickly become apparent to the rest of the organization. And they won't be committed either.

Norms

Norms explicitly define the preferred way to behave in a certain situation. The best organizations deliberately establish norms-- to guide and control their own behavior. The following norms have proven to be effective in crossing organizational boundaries.

- ***Leading-Across***

Leading across is a norm for dealing with conflicts between departments. The conflict may involve an outright disagreement, a change of plans that was not communicated, or one department not delivering agreed-upon services to another department.

Such conflicts are inevitable. Unfortunately most people aren't very good at dealing with them. Research indicates that two out of three people avoid conflict. By default, flight becomes the norm. As a result, minor concerns don't surface until they become major, costly problems—not good.

Norms for dealing with cross-functional conflict need to be explicit. The norm of "waving the flag" was developed by managers we worked with in Central Europe. It was effective because it gave conflict a voice. When conflict arose between two functions, each function was responsible for waving the flags:

- *Wave the White Flag*

This means - "I come in peace, don't shoot, let's talk." Conflict gets resolved at the level where it occurs. It is not avoided. It is not escalated to the next level. Managers do not allow their people to bring problems unless they have attempted to solve them at their level. "End-runs" are not tolerated.

- *Wave the Red Flag*

When an honest effort fails to resolve the conflict, it goes to the next level. The parties jointly do the escalation and present their case. They say, in effect, "We're stuck. We need your help. Here's the situation."

Waving the Flags became a helpful norm in a number of situations. For example, we found that cross-functional blaming often surfaced at monthly review meetings when one department was attempting to explain a negative variance. Once the norm was established, the leader's response to blaming became more pointed:

- *"So you've got a problem with another department? Did you go to them? If not, I've got a problem with you."*
- *"So you've got a problem with another department? You say you went to them and it still didn't work out? Then why didn't both of you bring it to me? I've got a problem with both of you."*

For this approach to work, the norm needs to be clear and the consequences swift. If conflict-avoidance is the path of least resistance, then the consequences need to be reversed. Reward those who uphold the norm and reprimand those that avoid it.

- ***Leading-Up***

Leading-up is a norm for resolving conflicts between levels. This might be a disagreement between a manager and his or her supervisor over roles, goals, or resources. Or it could relate to job satisfaction. Often it involves a simple misunderstanding.

The norm is simple - if you are not happy, lead-up. The acronym SCORE shows how leading-up works, with five key behaviors:

Situation - come prepared to explain the situation
Consequences - if no action is taken
Options - provide several solutions
Recommend a solution
Evaluate - identify how and when you will know if your solution is working.

For SCORE to be effective, managers at every level need to encourage and reward team members who lead-up. Team members also need to have the courage to lead-up, to come prepared to explain their problem and offer solutions.

Once leading-up is embedded in the culture, cross-level conflicts are usually solved in five to ten minutes. The manager who is leading-up usually has the first hand knowledge of the situation, and the manager's supervisor usually understands the broader strategic and organizational issues that might apply.

Equifax, a major provider of consumer credit information, has a leading-up norm called a put-up. It works this way. If you have a problem you cannot fix, you go to your supervisor with a recommended solution. If you complain to others, they will call you on it, and suggest you do a put-up. The implication is clear, put-up or shut-up.

Like many cultural elements, norms are essentially free. All they require is the imagination to create them and discipline to execute them.

Building Core Competencies

Whether you call it training, organizational development, or on-job coaching, the development of people is more than a good idea; it has become a strategic imperative.

Building core competencies becomes more critical in unstable times when products, tasks, and technologies are constantly changing. This is when the fundamentals matter most. We have found that a combination of three approaches is needed to build core competencies:

- ***Training*** -involves classroom or off-site workshops that provide participants with the skills to implement change back on the job. Large groups of people can acquire new skills in a short period of time. This is more efficient than individual coaching or an organizational development intervention. However, if new competencies acquired in a training class are not reinforced back on the job, they will be quickly lost. In addition, training is not the best solution for overcoming systemic problems.

- ***On-Job Coaching*** - places a major responsibility for developing people on the shoulders of line managers. It also puts managers on the front-lines where they can directly impact the execution of strategy. With on-job coaching, the transfer of learning is quick and direct. The effectiveness of the coaching can be evaluated directly by the improvement in performance. Unfortunately coaching tends to be a sacred cow that doesn't get fed. In companies that "get it," managers are supported, trained and held accountable for on-job coaching. It is an integral part of the performance management system, and will be discussed in chapter nine.

- ***Organizational Development (OD)*** - a disciplined approach to transforming the organization. It involves planned interventions guided by internal or external consultants, or even better by line managers with appropriate skills. OD involves assessing the current alignment of the organization and implementing the needed interventions, which is discussed throughout this book. In turbulent times, the ability to guide this process is an essential core competency for managers at all levels. A key advantage of OD is that it helps solve systemic problems, like the realignment of the *Three Points of Pressure.*

All three approaches - training, on-job coaching, and OD - have their advantages and disadvantages. Most major change interventions involve a mixture of the three. The challenge of course is to get the mix right.

Chapter Summary:

An enabling culture that supports the execution of strategy is composed of four indispensable elements:

- Leadership,
- Vision & Values
- Norms
- Core Competencies

COBRA-Scan employs various data gathering methods to assess the current culture. Then the appropriate interventions can be implemented.

A Culture of Discipline

A structured, step-by-step process is required to implement the interventions discussed in this book. This may involve acquiring new competencies, establishing a rigorous review process, or applying boundary management practices. The administrative effort--the planning, the coaching, and the monitoring--that is needed to internalize these interventions is significant. The best companies make the investment because they understand that once these interventions are embedded in the culture, they become self-perpetuating habits. The result is a culture of discipline that becomes second nature.

Chapter 4
Aligning the Structure

Structure: a roadblock or an expressway to market.

The structure of an organization is the formal arrangement of functions, levels, and processes, plus the roles and responsibilities for working within and across these arrangements. Structure is the second of the *Three Points of Pressure* that will be discussed. Strategy cannot be effectively executed unless structure is aligned.

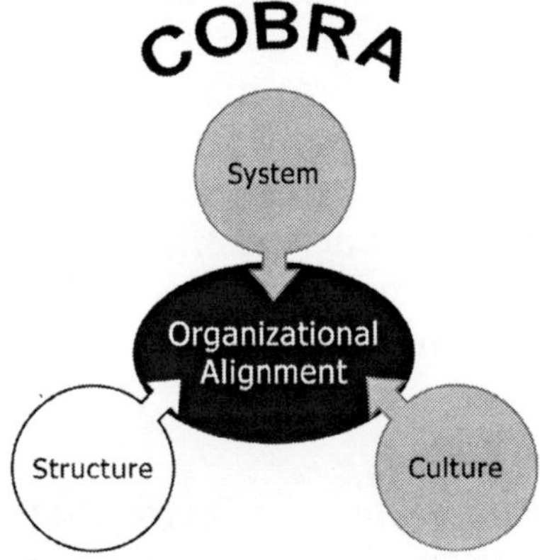

Structure can take many forms: a self-managed team, the traditional functional hierarchy, a matrix and more. It can be organized by trade channel, by product, by geography and so on. At its best, structure creates order and efficiency; at its worst it causes disruptive boundaries and collisions. When the structure is undermining the ability of the organization to execute the strategy, it usually involves one or more of the following factors:

1. Formal Structure: Does it provide both economies of scale and customer satisfaction?
2. Boundary Mgmt.: Are boundaries between functions/levels deliberately managed?

3. Core Processes: Are core business processes efficient and effective?
4. Bridging Structures: is bridging used to deal with complex issues?

This chapter will discuss change interventions that address each of these factors. If the structure of an organization is compared to a house, the formal structure is like the floor plan; boundary management equates to the doors and hallways that provide passage throughout the house; processes resemble the plumbing and electrical systems; and bridging structures are like ladders and scaffolding that are used to solve the occasional, extraordinary structural problem. The fifth section of this chapter will provide an example of a boundary intervention called *Maps and Mission.*

A word in advance - the first instinct of most leaders is to focus on changing the formal structure. In our experience, this is often the factor that needs the least attention. How interactions are managed across the boundaries is by far the paramount area of concern. Keep this in mind as we look more closely at each of the four factors.

1. Formal Structure

The formal structure is the first factor that we will discuss. It defines how functions and levels are arranged, that is, the look of the organization chart.

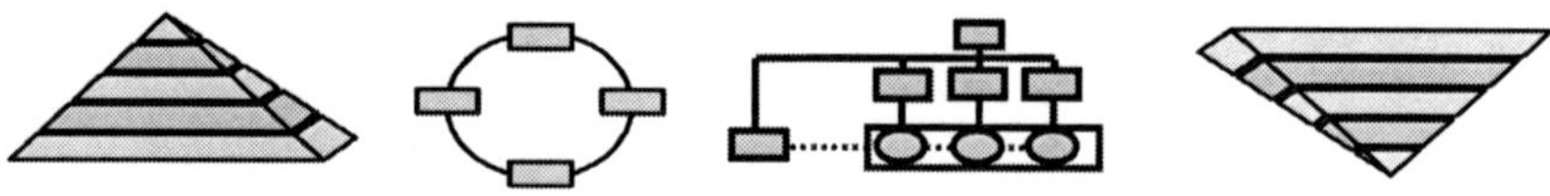

Changes in strategy trigger changes to the formal structure:

- If you are pursuing a low-cost strategy, it might make sense to consolidate satellite manufacturing operations into one highly efficient mega-plant, shifting from a local to a regional or multi-national structure.

- Conversely, an acquisition strategy involving a significant growth in the size of your market may trigger the need to shift from a centralized structure to a regional structure that provides more local autonomy.

- Fast-moving consumer goods companies often reach a point where they shift from a geographic sales structure to a trade channel structure to better serve the varying needs of their customers.

- Some organizations decide to become more vertically integrated in pursuing a low-cost strategy. In the beverage industry, this might involve producing your own packaging or manufacturing your own coolers and display racks. When well executed, vertical integration can drive down costs significantly, but structurally it adds more functions and boundaries.

Companies that aspire to be major global players usually adopt a strategy of bigger is better. Large companies benefit from improved purchasing power and economies of scale. They are also in a better position to serve larger customers.

Yet much of what we know about organizational effectiveness suggests that smaller is better. The challenge of course is to gain the benefits of size without becoming centralized and bureaucratic. Scale without autonomy is generally stifling. As companies grow larger, they need to explore ways to divide into smaller, simpler arrangement to gain speed and agility.

Don't let division become subtraction

Such sub-divisions, however, have their own dangers. They can fragment accountability for a complete task and create boundary issues. For example, some manufacturing operations have experimented with two supervisors per line as they added more shifts and lines. This involved one supervisor having responsibility for the front-end of multiple lines, and a second having responsibility for the back-end of multiple lines. It looked good on paper because the total number of supervisors and the cost of goods are reduced. Unfortunately in practice, it creates an artificial boundary in the middle of a complete task. Line efficiencies went down and costs went up. Most operations reverted to the one supervisor per line structure, where the supervisor had control and accountability for the complete output of the line. The increased efficiencies more than paid for the additional supervisors.

Troubled companies often jump on restructuring as a quick-fix for all organizational problems. This is human nature, not just a modern habit. Even the ancients couldn't resist redrawing their org charts.

"Every time we were beginning to form up into teams, we would be reorganized. I was to learn later in life that we tend to meet any new situation by reorganization; and a wonderful method it can be for creating the illusion of progress while producing confusion, inefficiency, and demoralization."

Attributed to Petronius Arbitor, 50 AD

Yet even when you get the formal structure the way you want it, you will probably end up with some form of the functional hierarchy. In its simplest form, levels of authority cascade down from the top, and technically specialized disciplines are organized into functions. This is the most common business structure for good reason - it usually works better than alternatives.

And if functional hierarchies were favored in the past, they are even more compelling today. This is because consumers are smarter and more demanding. They want it all: quality, value, service. Product differentiation, low cost operations, speed-to-market, and customer service are near universal priorities. So the task of producing and delivering competitive products and services becomes more and more complicated. Complexity in product development, supply chain, and customer service creates the need for more specialized technology and expertise, which calls for functional groupings. In fact, as markets become more competitive, each functional area within a company is competing with its functional counterparts in other companies, trying to be faster, better and cheaper. To fail is to run the risk of being outsourced.

No matter how you arrange the boxes on the org chart or draw the lines of responsibility, there will always be boundaries separating functions and levels. This brings us to the all-important task of assessing how well those boundaries are managed.

2. Boundary Management

Boundary management deals with how people work across the formal structure. It involves aligning roles, goals, and working relationships to create a common purpose.

Each function has a dual responsibility to the organization: to deliver productivity within their function, and to deliver customer satisfaction across functional lines. Think of a track-and-field relay. The runner is responsible for running his or her leg of the race, but also handing the baton to the next runner. Fumbling the handoff almost guarantees losing the race. The same is true in a company. And when a baton drops, it usually happens on the boundaries. So this is where more attention should be focused. But usually it is not.

You will recall the term "disruptive boundaries" used earlier. It is a contact point between functional areas or different levels where batons drop with regularity. In our experience, disruptive boundaries are the most common structural problem found in a company. When a COBRA-Scan identifies this problem, two boundary management interventions are generally needed.

- Customer Maps and Mission— break down disruptive boundaries between functions.

- The Point of Control—breaks down disruptive boundaries between levels.

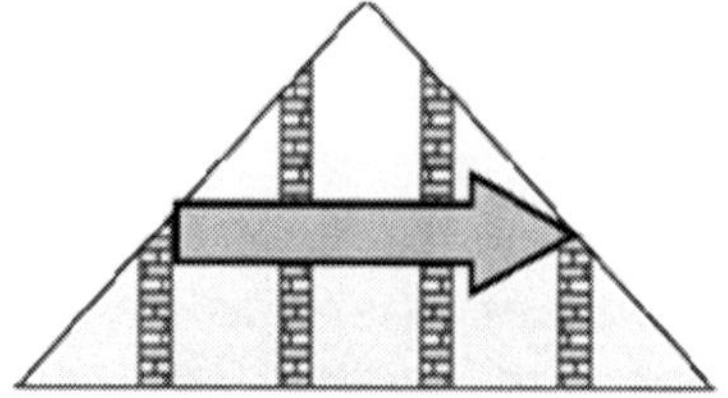

Customer Maps and Mission

Customer Maps and Mission bring the supplier-customer discipline of the open market inside the organization. Each function receives products or services from their external or internal suppliers and delivers these products or services to their internal or final customers. Think of the organization as a chain of customers with each function adding value to the final product or service that is delivered to the final customer.[1]

With Customer Maps, we identify the internal or final customer of each function, and the products or services it provides to each customer. The Mission explicitly defines cross-functional roles and responsibilities. Section 5 of this chapter explores Customer Maps and Mission in more depth.

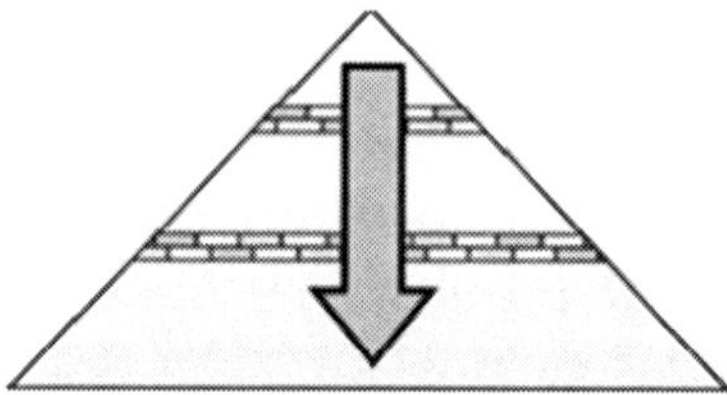

The Point of Control

Just as some form of functional grouping is here to stay, so too are groupings by level. While functions are more about task; levels are more about power. Levels divide organizations into manageable chunks based on internal or customer grouping and the limits of span of control. They define the decision making authority at each level, and clarify who is in charge, who reports to whom, and where "the buck stops." When it comes to authority and accountability things need to be kept as clear and simple as possible.

The concept of Point of Control grew out of Open Systems Theory[2] but has surely been around forever. Simply stated, competent people closest to the action are in the best position to control the action—to respond to fast-breaking problems and opportunities. They usually understand the situation better: the concrete details, the personalities, the constraints. They are also in a position to take timely action and to learn by trial and error. It is hard to argue with this, yet large hierarchical organizations have a way of getting it wrong.

The explosion of the Challenger space shuttle is a tragic example of what can happen when control is located too far from where work occurs. The Challenger exploded on takeoff, killing all onboard because of an o-ring failure. A US Senate investigation revealed that engineers at lower levels were aware of the risk and discouraged the launch. However NASA's senior managers in Washington, where launch decisions were made, didn't fully understand the risk and had another agenda. Politically, a successful mission was required. The investigation concluded that:

Those with the power lacked the information, and those with the information lacked the power.

The same description applies to many large, multi-level organizations. The objective of Point of Control is to shift the management of work - planning, problem-solving and decision-making - as close as possible to where the work occurs. This is more important than ever in a fast-moving global environment. As Edward Lawler III has pointed out, four factors are required to empower teams at lower levels.[3] They are illustrated in chart 2.

Chart 2

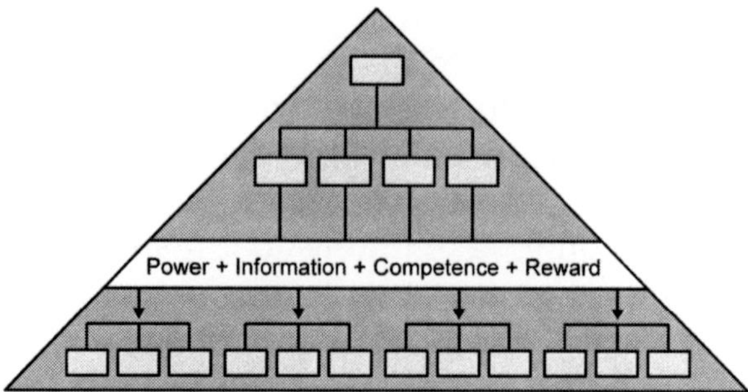

1. Power—they need the authority to make decision related to managing performance at their level
2. Information—they need to be involved; they need timely information on actual performance versus target
3. Competence--they need the competence to manage performance: planning, problems solving, decision making
4. Reward--they need to be rewarded for managing rather than just following orders

There will always be some decisions that must be made centrally. Yet when done properly, moving the Point of Control closer to the action enables large, multi-level organizations to stay street-smart, street-quick, and customer focused. In chapter 6 we will discuss a concept called Managing the Red Box, which is a COBRA methodology for moving control closer to the action. Section 4 of chapter 7 also provides a process for providing more autonomy to lower levels.

3. Process Improvement

This is the third structural intervention that will be discussed. Processes operate within and across functions and have a major impact on productivity and customer satisfaction.

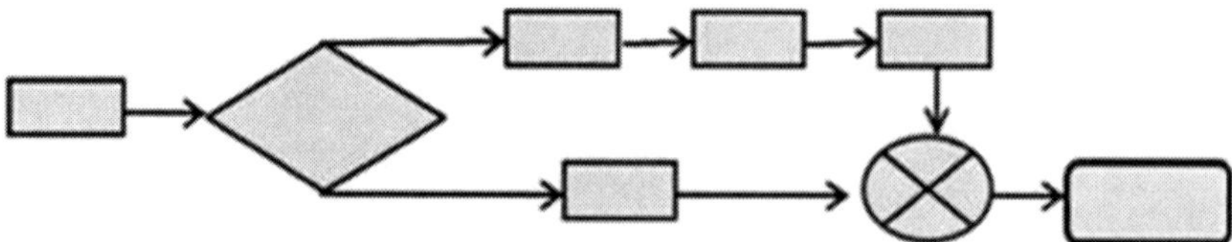

The following are examples of core processes, all of which involve many boundary crossings:

- New Product Development
- Sales Forecasting—Production Planning
- Promotional Planning and Execution
- Order Entry and Delivery
- Invoicing and Cash Collection
- Accounts Receivable
- Selection and Development of People

After boundary management, process improvement is the intervention most needed by the companies we work with. Processes become ineffective for various reasons:

- Too linear, non-branching --the goal of creating one, bullet-proof, all encompassing process to handle every conceivable contingency leads instead to a bureaucratic black hole.

- Too many sign-offs--becoming so internally "process-pure" that the organization can't deliver to customers. And when customers complain, they are subjected to the most maddening of responses, "I am just doing my job."

- Process overload--the sheer volume and complexity of work overloads the current process.

- Outdated technology --new technology is not exploited.

The following case illustrates the importance of integrating process improvement and boundary management interventions. This client was fortunate to have executive-level commitment.

Heat and Light

It was day two of an off-site I was facilitating, and we were stuck. The management team of the Hellenic Bottling Company had assembled in Patras, Greece to improve the product development process for Amita, a new local juice brand. The products were excellent but the development cycle was too long. Competitors often got wind of new products under development and were able to preempt the launch with their own promotional activities.

The previous day we had identified each step of the current development process. Detailed process flow charts now hung from every wall. The atmosphere in the room was toxic—a bitter blend of tobacco and testosterone. Our analysis had identified a process that was Homeric in complexity, over 120 separate steps in the process, involving over fifty boundary crossings. We had got that far and no further, the glimmer of a technical solution strangled by cross-functional conflict. To proceed would require that people from different departments work together for the common good.

Tito Komninos, the General Manager, dropped by that morning to assess our progress. After listening to arguments and counter-arguments for thirty minutes, he stepped to the front of the room. Tito had a fine feel for the difference between heat and light. Reigning -in his frustration, he spoke in his best Don Corleone whisper, "Surely we can do better than this." Though coded, everyone got the message. He then walked to the back of the room and quietly observed. Within four hours we had redesigned the process—going from 120 steps to 80 and reducing the number of boundary crossing from 50 to 27. More importantly we had the beginnings of a collaborative work team.

This is the kind of boundary-bashing that often needs to be part of streamlining a business process. Today Amita has nineteen flavours, a 60% share of the Greek market, and is widely distributed throughout Europe.

Process improvement and boundary management are similar but different. Sometimes the process itself is the cause of an unaligned structure, and sometimes unmanaged boundaries impair a well designed process. Both need to be carefully assessed before implementing a change.

4. Bridging Structure

This is the fourth type of structural intervention. Bridging structures are mechanisms for dealing with extraordinary, non-programmable work between functions and levels. They can involve:

- A temporary project team to deal with a major change initiative, such as a new product introduction

- A permanent cross-functional team to manage a complex process like sales forecasting and production planning.

- A "process czar" to ensure each function is doing its part in optimizing core business processes.

- A strategic alliance with a supplier or customer.

Bridging structures enabled Cisco Systems to "hot wire" its formal structure. After the company wrote off $2.2 billion in losses, CEO John Chambers...*"realized that the company's hierarchical structure precluded it from moving quickly into new markets, so he began to group executives into cross-functional-teams...Chambers used just three words to describe the benefits...'speed, skill, and flexibility'."* [4]

The common boss is another important bridging structure.[5] One of the roles of the common boss is to manage the interface between sub-units that report to them. The operations manager illustrated in chart 4 is the common boss of the production, warehouse, and distribution managers.

Chart 4

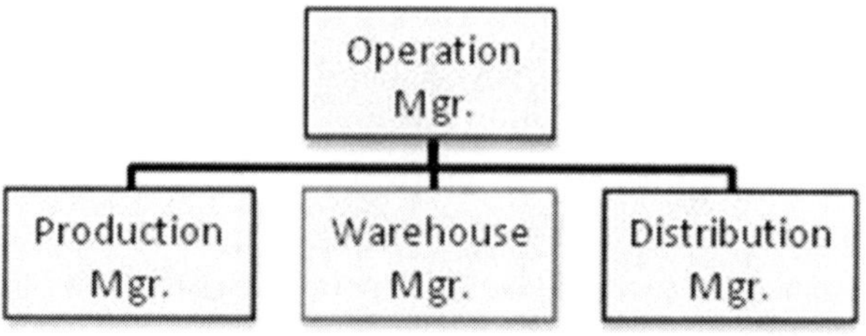

There is nothing new about the role of the common boss. It is built into the authority of most organization. It is what good managers are expected to do. Some like Marcel are better than others.

> ***Coffee with Marcel***
>
> Marcel was the operations manager in a Romanian plant. He regularly wandered through the production, warehouse and loading areas... watching, listening and chatting informally. He also closely monitored daily performance measures for each of his sub-units. If you saw Marcel at your office door with a cup of coffee in his hand you knew something was up. One day I observed Marcel approaching the warehouse supervisor's office, he said, *"grab a cup of coffee and let's go down to the production supervisor's office."* Later I noticed the warehouse supervisor and the production supervisor shaking hands as the meeting ended--very low-key, very professional. Marcel had a knack for detecting the itch before the scratch.

5. Customer Maps & Mission:

By now you will recognize that we believe cross-functional and cross-level boundary issues are not only the most common structural impediment to alignment - but also the most obstinate. So the balance of this chapter is devoted to overcoming this problem, using our Customer Maps & Mission intervention.

Most companies have an organization chart that neatly divides the business into levels and functions. Few, however, have defined how all these pieces fit together to create a common purpose. Customer Maps & Mission are designed to bridge this gap, to help each function define its functional and cross-functional responsibilities. They describe why each function exists, who it serves, and how it supports the organization. They are underpinned by roles, performance measures and consequences. There are five steps in the Maps and Mission intervention:

- Mapping Customers, Products and Services: Identify internal or final customers that your unit serves and the current products and services you provide to each of your customers.

- Customer Requirements: Interview each customer to determine its needs and requirements.

- Supplier Requirements: As a supplier, you share your unit's requirements with each of your customers, what you need from your customer in order to provide excellent products and services.

- Boundary Changes: A mutual agreement on what your unit and your customer need to stop doing (work-out) and what you need to start doing (work-in) to improve customer service.

- Functional Changes: Identifies what your unit needs to change within your function that will enable you to deliver on boundary agreements.

Step 1 – Mapping Customers, Products and Service

Here you identify your unit's customers and the products and/or services you provide to each, as shown in chart 5 below. This example comes from the Quality Assurance (QA) Department in a typical beverage operation. It identifies the department's three customers, the services performed for each, and the approximate time and effort involved in delivering each of the services. As you see, approximately half of QA's time and effort is dedicated to the Production Department.

Chart 5

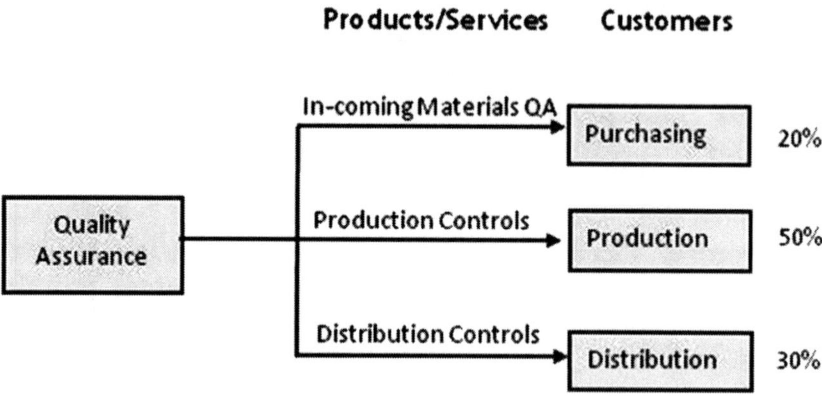

Chart 5 is a work flow map, which is the most common type of customer map. Products and services flow downstream from the purchase of raw materials, to finished goods, to the delivery of products or services to the final customer.

If you compare this type of map with the way an organization's structure is usually depicted – a pyramid showing groupings of functions and levels - something interesting becomes obvious. The traditional pyramid leaves out the customer, the product/service, and the work flow.

By arranging each unit map in the sequence of the work flow, a very different way of viewing the organization emerges – horizontal and cross-functional instead of hierarchical and function-centric. Chart 6 below shows this approach in a simplified view of a typical manufacturing and sales operation.

Chart 6

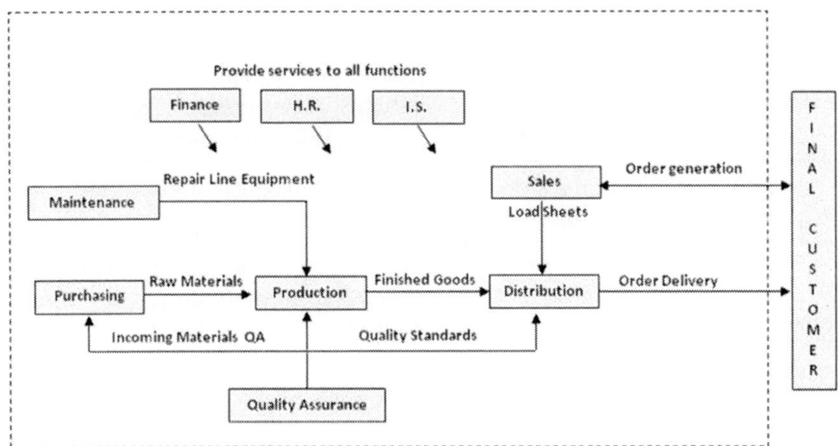

This display is more useful than a static pyramid in capturing how products and services move across the organization to the final customer. The real work of the organization comes into view – what happens, who does it, how it fits together.

Continuing with the mapping in a more detailed manner, critical information emerges about the relative weight of different activities. Chart 7 illustrates the approximate percentage of time and effort a supplier devotes to different functions in order to satisfy the customer's requirements. This is based on an analysis of a typical week.

Chart 7

Supplier	***Customer***	***Product/Service***
Purchasing	60% Production 35% Sales	Raw and package materials Sales assets
Quality Assurance	20% Purchasing 50% Production 30% Distribution	Incoming goods control Production/Distribution controls
Maintenance	70% Production 30% Other Functions	Repair and maintain line equipment and utilities.

Production	95% Distribution	Produce finished goods based on schedule.
Distribution	90% Retail customers	Store and load finished goods on trucks, order delivery, & collect returnable packages.
Sales	95% Retail customers	Order generation and market development
H.R.	All functions	Recruiting, selection, training, salary admin., benefits, etc.
Finance	40% Sales 30% Other Functions	P & L by department, payment, budgets, etc.
I.S.	All functions	Maintain systems, hardware and software development

To deliver products and service to the final customer each link in the chain needs to do its part. Chart 8 illustrates how each link operates:

Chart 8

The supplier's role is to deliver the needed products and services based on the customer's requirements. The customer's role is to communicate its requirements and to provide feedback on any changes to requirements. Not surprisingly, the two most common causes of customer service breakdowns are: the customer did not communicate its requirements or changes to requirements, or the supplier did not deliver what was agreed on. This supplier/customer interface is exactly where disruptive boundaries are created or eliminated. This is where execution succeeds or fails.

In spite of the old adage, the customer isn't always right. The customer has to "give-to-get." If the customer fails to give the supplier information on requirements or changes to requirements, then the customer may not get the service they expect. Conversely if the customer's requirements are accurate and the supplier does not deliver, then the supplier owns the problem and needs to fix it. At this level of detail we can identify specific roles and requirements and quickly analyze problems. Chart 9 defines the roles that suppliers and customers need to adopt to optimize customer service across the organization.

Chart 9

Role of Supplier	***Role of Customer***
• Understand your customer's needs • Deliver!--provide goods and services that satisfy these needs. • Stay in contact with customers--know when their needs change. • Speak-up if you are not getting what you need from your customers. Wave the White Flag! (see chapter 2) • "Own the problem" ...take the initiative to solve problems regardless of who dropped the baton.	• Communicate your unit's needs • Understand supplier's constraints. Be reasonable, be flexible • Provide your suppliers with the information they need to serve your unit--Give to Get! • Speak-up when you are not satisfied with the service you are receiving from your suppliers. Wave the White Flag!

Most disruptive boundaries start as small issues that become larger and more complex because they are overlooked or avoided. Once the roles of the supplier and customer are clarified and internalized most problems can be solved quickly and easily.

This is an extremely important first step in building a network of working relationships across the organization, especially in companies where functional roles and goals predominate. This is often an uncomfortable but transforming experience for traditional managers.

Step 2: Customer Requirements

This brings us to the second step of Customer Maps and Mission. At this point each unit has completed a customer map identifying each of its customers and the products or service being provided. The units have presented their maps to the overall team and made any needed corrections.

Now, the map information is entered on a Maps and Mission Worksheet, shown in chart 10. Columns 1, 2, and 3 are our focus at this point - we will come to the other columns shortly.

Maps and Mission Worksheet

Unit: Warehouse

1. Customer	2. Current Products/ Services	3. Customer Require-ments (Distribu-tion)	4. Supplier Require-ments (Ware-house)	5. Boundary Changes	
				Work-Out	Work-In
Distribution Function	Load and Unload Goods	Loading time per truck—per standard by truck type	Teach driv-ers Good Manufactur-ing Practices (GMP)	Stop leaving pallets, car-tons, plastic wraps in truck.	Require-ments are clear, we need to get better at measure and manag-ing
		All trucks must be loaded for 1st routes by 7:00A	Timely submit load sheets to Warehouse		Load sheet part 1 by 16:00, part 2 by 23:30, night loads by 20:00

		Trucks are driven to warehouse during daytime by WHS staff			Additional WHS workers discussed with HR, Jan 2005
		Load is accurate, countable, conveniently placed in trucks, and safe for transportation.	Daily information on loading errors or violations	Stop closing truck bays/ doors with forklifts.	Meet together regularly to review loading time, accuracy and effectiveness. Develop simple, safe rules for loading trucks
		Report on retuned breakage	Driver should inform gate checker for reason of full goods returned.		Incorporate changes to procedure for exchanging breakage in outlets.
		Loading time for 2nd and 3rd routes—30 min. per truck	Schedule of 2nd and 3rd routes		All in place
		Report on night loading to DSD by 7:00A			All in place

6. Functional Changes	
• **Improve management system** (key indicators, tracking review)? *Regular 5 minute daily review*	• **Training/Coaching?** *Training on inventory management*
• **Improve functional job design/processes**? *Improve order picking process*	• **Functional communication?**
• **Technology?** *N/A*	• **Other?**

Now, each supplier sits down with one of its customers and discusses the customer's requirements. The supplier needs to ask good, probing questions, to listen carefully, and to understand the reality of the customer's business. These topics should be covered:

- Satisfaction with the relationship?
- Requirements?
- Constraints?

As Jerry Maguire says in the film by the same name, "Help me help you." That is the attitude of the supplier in this discussion (or should be.)

On the matter of customer constraints, what do we mean? Our approach in working with clients is to ask internal customers how much of their work they can plan and control. When we ask this of production managers, the usual response is around 80%. For sales managers, the usual response is around 50%. Why such a gap? Sales units are constantly trying to meet the needs of the company's external customers,--usually in a volatile, competitive market. If production managers understand this reality, they are less likely to resist last minute changes, and more likely to build contingencies into their production plans. In an increasingly turbulent marketplace, everyone in the company has to cope with uncertainty and change, while still meeting performance standards.

Customer requirements are entered in Column 3 of the worksheet. Chart 10 gives an example of what the Distribution Unit (customer) requires of the Warehouse Unit (supplier).

Step 3: Supplier Requirements

It's a two-way street, of course. Once the customer's requirements are understood, the supplier sets forth its requirements. Now it is the responsibility of the customer to understand the supplier's requirements and constraints. The customer takes its turn asking good questions, listening carefully, and working to understand the reality of the supplier's business.

Column 4 of chart 10 shows what the Warehouse unit requires of the Distribution unit in order to serve them well. Notice that three of the supplier's requirements deal with providing information or feedback to the supplier. This is what we referred to earlier as "give to get"...providing the supplier with what it needs to serve you well.

Step 4: Boundary Changes

The supplier-customer discussion is not over – in fact, it's just getting to the good part. Next they move to boundary issues – what needs to change in order to improve their working relationship and the end result for the company.

It is very likely that boundary issues already will have surfaced as the supplier and customer talk through their respective requirements. But even if no problems have entered the conversation, the parties should deliberately focus on changes that are needed to meet all requirements on both sides.

There are disciplined ways to identify and work through the boundary issues. We are indebted to the General Electric Company for the work-out/work-in approach discussed below.

Work-Out: Refers to anything you are currently doing for a customer or a supplier that is no longer necessary. You need to stop doing these things, that is, work them out of the system.

An enormous amount of time and energy is wasted in doing things that no longer add value.

In some cases the customer's requirements have changed over time, yet certain processes, procedures or reports are still in effect. In other cases, bad habits have crept in, such as avoiding conflict --blaming but not confronting. Work-Out identifies what needs to be stopped.

Work-In: Work-In is about starting. Once you have a clear idea of your customer's or supplier's requirements, you have the opportunity to work-in to the relationship anything that will enhance internal productivity and customer satisfaction. This may involve:

- Major or minor changes to the current product or service. For example, rather than just delivering a financial report to your customer, expand the service by consulting with them to ensure they understand and can act on the report.

- More structured communication and feedback between units

- Better problem solving skills

- Major changes to the other fundamentals: the system, or the culture

Chart 11 illustrates the Work-In, Work-Out process. The vertical column represents the work performed by the supplier in providing the current products and services to each customer, the status-quo. The horizontal row represents what the customer actually needs, which has been uncovered in the previous dialogue. Together, the supplier and the customer need to work-out those things that are no longer needed and work-in those things that are.

Chart 11

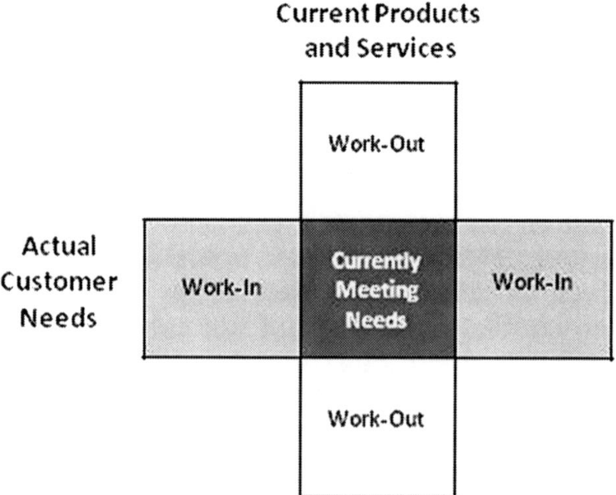

Returning to our worksheet, column 5 of chart 10 shows what the Warehouse and the Distribution department will *stop* doing and what they will *start* doing. Yes there will be additional work but unproductive work will be eliminated--a fair trade-off.

Step 5: Functional Changes

At this point, the customer and supplier have identified boundary changes that are needed. Now each can focus on how to effect change within its own function in order to deliver on the new boundary agreements. This involves exploring ways to improve products or services delivered to the customer - the quality, the productivity, the speed, the cost, or some other attribute. As indicated on the worksheet this may involve improving:

- Performance management system
- Job design or functional processes
- Technology
- Training/ coaching

Section 6 of chart 10 identifies three things the warehouse (supplier) commits to changing in order to improve functional performance: regular 5 minute daily review meeting for each warehouse shift team, improve the order picking process, and training on inventory management.

Keeping the Boundaries Open

While the Customer Maps & Mission intervention can be employed to solve a specific boundary problem, it also creates a "contract" that serves to keep the boundaries permanently open. It is difficult to overstate the importance of building a collaborative relationship between suppliers and customers.

"The greatest opportunity for performance improvements often lies in the functional interfaces -- those points at which the baton is being passed from one department to another" [6]

Boundary problems are inevitable. Both parties will be at fault at one time or another. It is critical, therefore, to get problems on the table early. TARP International has done extensive research on internal and final customer satisfaction. They consistently find the following:

"The average business never hears from 96% of its unhappy customers." [7]

If most unhappy customers do not complain, then suppliers need to take the initiative in monitoring their satisfaction. This, as they say, is a no-brainer.

TARP also found that, *"up to 70% of customers that actually complain will do business again if the complaint is resolved."* Again the implication is clear. If we do a good job of handling unhappy customers, we stand a very good chance of regaining their trust, cooperation and business. The first step in solving service problems however is in knowing they exist.

Nothing can replace regular face-to-face contact, walking down the hall and asking your customer, "Are you getting everything you need from us?"

Chapter Summary:

When the structure is undermining the ability of the organization to execute the strategy, it usually involves one or more of the following:

Structure: Keys to Execution

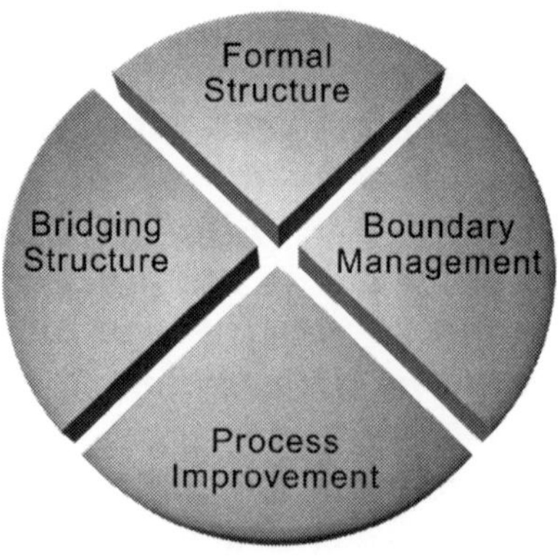

- Formal Structure: does it provide scale economies and customer satisfaction?
- Boundary Management: are boundaries deliberately managed?
- Core Processes: are core processes simple, streamlined and cost-effective?
- Bridging Structure: is bridging used with complex, structural issues?

We recommend you move in descending order in implementing change. If the formal structure is a problem, it should be corrected first, or it will undermine the other three factors. Once the formal structure has been changed or eliminated as a possible problem; move on to boundary management interventions. Unmanaged boundaries, not the formal structure, are the most common and persistent problem we run into. The two boundary interventions that are most often needed are: Customer Maps & Mission, and pushing management down to the Point of Control.

Once boundaries are being managed, move on to improve processes or to introduce bridging structures. Process or bridging issues are often symptoms of problems caused by the formal structure or unmanaged boundaries. Chapter 5 will discuss the performance management system.

Chapter 5
Aligning the System

The system is the great flywheel of execution.

A company's performance management system guides the planning and execution of strategy. The system is the third of the *Three Points of Pressure*.

All organizations have some type of system to manage performance. It is remarkable, however, how often the system can breakdown by becoming too complex, too centralized, or too slow. In working with clients, we often find a flawed system cluttered with oversight controls.

The following elements can be useful in managing performance, but they are not a management system:

- Formal planning process
- A top-down control system
- A monthly P&L report
- A book of key indicators
- An elaborate information system
- Benchmarking
- A performance appraisal program
- Management by Objectives driven down functional lines

Some of these elements will be found in a well designed performance management system. Others actually get in the way.

The Power of Simplicity and Discipline

Effective systems are simple and disciplined. Simple, however, is rarely easy.

- Making things complicated is easy ... keeping them simple is hard.

- Analyzing a performance problem from behind a desk is easy ... getting out to the "sharp end" to solve it is hard.

- Avoiding conflict is easy ... directly dealing with it is hard.

- Jumping to a solution is easy...ferreting out the root cause of a problem is hard.

- "Exception-reporting" is easy ... regular face-to-face reviews are hard.

Operating a simple, disciplined system has never been easy--it just happens to produce great results.

This chapter will discuss:

1. Five Components of the System
2. Five Attributes of the System
3. Common System Problems
4. Building the System

****

1. The Five Components of a Simple, Disciplined System

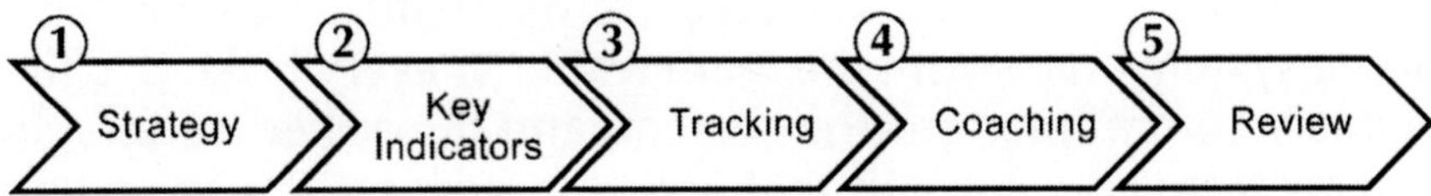

The best systems have five components working together like the fingers of a hand. They are simple in design and disciplined in execution.

System Design	*System Execution*
1. Strategy Defines overall direction of company and business unit.	• Communicating strategy in simple language to all levels. • "Lighthouse Surveillance" of environment for emerging opportunities and competitive threats • Realign strategy to market changes
2. Key Indicators Translates strategy into measurable action.	• Continuously testing to ensure that key indicators are measuring the right things in the simplest way. • Realigning key indicators to changes of strategy • Balanced metrics: functional productivity and cross-functional customer service, etc.
3. Tracking Timely and accurate information on actual performance.	• Exploiting new information technology in tracking hard, quantifiable indicators. • Finding simple ways to measure soft, qualitative indicators.
4. Coaching Line managers provide on-job coaching.	• Real-time, performance improvement • Enables managers to get out on the job and monitor soft indicators, and to maintain regular contact with customers
5. Review Face to face review of key indicators versus targets.	• Review performance for period, rewarding results, solving problems, etc • Evaluate YTD strategy execution and revise strategy or tactics as required • Develop coaching plans for performance variances caused by skill-gaps

The design provides the basic structure and integrity of the system. The five components need to be aligned with one another and tailored to the needs of the team. The execution of the system starts with the team leader at every level. It is the leader's commitment to the system, and his or her leadership and problem solving skills that drive the system. The execution needs to be both loose and tight: loose in adapting the system to an ever-changing business environment, and tight in the disciplined application of the five components.

The five components are very interdependent. A change in one factor triggers the need for a change in the others. They need to be managed separately and collectively. We will see in a later section of this chapter how each component is developed.

2. Five Attributes of a Simple, Disciplined System

The best systems have five attributes in common.

The System links the Planning and Execution of the Strategy.

A common flaw of ineffective systems is that they focus more on planning than on execution. The planning and execution are tightly linked in the five component system. The system is like a bicycle.

The strategy, key indicators, and tracking system provide the plans and overall direction--the front wheel of the bike. On-job coaching and performance review provide the energy and discipline to execute the strategy--the back wheel of the bike. Coaching gets managers out on the job where they can directly influence execution. The review process continuously assesses current performance against planned performance. It determines, for example, if a break-down is caused by faulty planning or faulty execution. When the planning and execution are linked you have an effective system--an early warning system.

Few would argue with what is required to build an effective performance management system:

- The strategy is aligned with the environment.
- Strategic objectives are translated into actionable key indicators.
- Responsibility and accountability are crystal clear at every level.
- Performance is regularly monitored on the job and reviewed with the team.
- Rewards and consequences are linked to results.
- And of course, effective leaders are needed to operate the system

Nevertheless these factors challenge many organizations. A recent survey of the senior executives of 197 global companies with sales exceeding $500 million found the following:

"Companies typically realize 60% of their strategies' potential value because of defects and breakdowns in planning and execution." [1]

Chart 2 identifies where the performance was lost. As you can see most of the losses were the results of an ineffective performance management system.

Chart 2

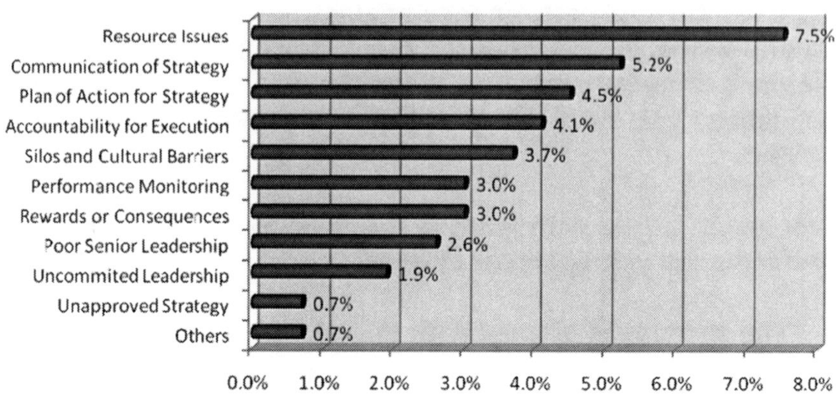

The System operates across all Levels and Functions.

The second attribute involves alignment. Plans, measures and reviews must be aligned from the top-down and from the bottom up. If the system isn't working at the supervisory level, it will fail. And if it isn't working at higher levels, it has no chance of working at the supervisory level. As we discussed in the last chapter, the goal is to move decision-making as close as possible to the point of action.

In addition, the system needs to operate across functions, at those critical interfaces where each department passes the baton to an internal or final customer. This horizontal dimension of the system helps to keep functional boundaries open.

The System creates Positive Performance Pressure.

It is easy to squeeze the life out of a system if you get too heavy handed. This is often the case when the system is imposed from the top and used as a hammer.

People can be very elusive if they are trapped into performing. The fascinating thing is that most people really thrive on challenge when they are fully engaged. The best way to create positive performance pressure is to involve the team in building and operating the system.

It is normal for there to be a lot of healthy "pushing and shoving" when it comes to reaching agreement on plans, measures and standards. Fight fair, make a case for your position, but leave the room with a common commitment.

Finally the system needs to hold people accountable for results. This calls for leaders who can apply the right balance of heat and light in executing the plan. Some performance problems call for light--understanding, communication and coaching. Others call for heat—increased performance pressure and imposing consequences. Most problems call for a bit of both.

To achieve great performance, people need to feel the system is fair and reasonable, and that they have a measure of control over the outcome. Our firm has found again and again that both productivity and motivation improve when people have clear direction, appropriate levels of freedom, regular performance feedback and equitable rewards and recognition.

The System is Mandatory.

In the film *Dead Poets Society* Robin Williams asks his students to walk around a garden path. Some stride, some lag, some shuffle. But when he turns on the music, they quickly fall into step.

A good system is like that. Once a team gets into the rhythm of planning, executing and reviewing performance, it becomes second nature. They are in control.

Never-the-less, we have yet to see an effective system operating across all levels and functions that evolved voluntarily.

Optional systems tend to wind down over time.

As mentioned earlier, the system needs to be loose and tight. This is the tight part. In most organizations, delivering results is enough—*show me the numbers*—and you are a winner. If the outcome is good, executing the system is "nice to have" but of secondary importance.

The best organizations are more demanding. Yes, by all means—*show me the numbers...but in addition, show me the system*. Show me the system that will enable you to deliver results today, and that also will enable you to sustain high performance in the future. This requires that you manage the system at your level and monitor the system at the level below you.

A Street Fighter and System Builder

Tony Maher, the field sales manager of six Eastern European countries, is a Kerryman with wings. He generally plans his field visits to coincide with each sales team's weekly or monthly performance review. Team leaders are never sure, however, when he is coming. The first day or so is spent in the market. He doesn't miss much: execution against standard, competitive activity, customer issues, consumer behavior. If things are going well you will hear about it, and if they aren't, he is out there with you getting it right.

So yeah, Tony is a hands-on, street fighter. But he understands that an effective management system is needed to drive market execution. On each visit he also sits-in review meeting--checking to see that they are measuring the right things, testing their tracking system, helping to analyze and solve problems.

Some managers make regular market visits, and some are good at analyzing results in a review meeting. Tony does both. He knows both approaches have limits but the combination gives him the total picture, and also gives him the opportunity to assess two critical skill sets. He wants the system to work when he is there, but more importantly he wants it to work when he is not there.

You can't have a simple system unless you have a disciplined system. It's a hand in glove proposition. Ad hoc, discretionary systems tend to wind down or drift in the direction of complexity and bureaucracy, especially when they are not delivering results.

The System ties Rewards to Results.

If rewards don't reflect results, you run the risk of turning-off your good people and running-off your best people. Effective rewards are clearly understood, equitable, and competitive.

A well constructed management system will help you do this. Once strategic objectives and key indicators are clearly defined and accountability is understood (steps 1 & 2 of the system), you are in a position to determine how you will reward your people. The performance tracking and review (steps 3 and 5 of the system) will provide you with information on actual results compared to target or goal. Thus the system provides management with objective performance data for determining rewards.

Rewards can be tied to various kinds of results: functional productivity, corporate productivity, customer service, growth in core competencies, living the values, crossing boundaries, and so on. As indicated above, we recommend that you reward managers for delivering the numbers, and also for faithfully executing the system that delivers the numbers. Chapter 7 will provide suggestions on ways to measure and reward the execution of the system.

3. Common Problems with Management Systems

We have seen a variety of ineffective systems, and most are only a change or two away from coming into alignment and supporting strong execution. The following are examples of ineffective systems we have encountered:

Overly-Centralized System

The planning, problem solving, and decision making are concentrated at the executive level, far from the execution arena. Overly centralized systems create needless hierarchy and are slow in responding to emerging problems and opportunities--certainly not an early warning system.

Three-Component System

A three-component system seeks to gain control by managing the numbers from behind a desk. It is a remote control system, similar to overly centralized systems but found at any level of the organization. It is characterized by elaborate plans, numerous key indicators, and robust tracking systems. Less emphasis is given to on-job coaching and performance review.

As a consequence, this type of system is less effective at managing strategy execution.

Functional System

It works effectively down functional lines but not across them. Such systems focus on maximizing functional productivity at the expense of systems productivity and customer satisfaction. They unintentionally foster functional silos.

Undisciplined System

These systems are often well designed, but poorly executed. The responsible team leader--whether in the boardroom or on the shop floor--lacks the competence and/or courage to manage the system. Some are ineffective coaches and motivators. Some are ineffective problem solvers and decision makers. And some just aren't demanding enough in dealing with chronic under-achievers. Without discipline, simple systems become complex and ineffective.The team in the following case avoided the common problems of management systems. Here's how it happened.

4. Case: Building a Simple Disciplined System

This case describes how the management system of a Customer Service Center (CSC) was built. The CSC is a national telephone sales group, a sub-unit of the organization's sales function. At the time we assessed its effectiveness, the group had been in operation for two years. Prior to that, order-generation was done directly by the field sales group. By any industry standard, this CSC team was highly effective.

Mission/Strategy

The CSC team was actively involved in the strategic planning and the development of the system. Team members visited CSC operations in other countries to observe best practices. Then they drafted a unit mission statement which provided answers to some very basic questions: Why does our unit exist? Who do we serve (see customer map below). How do we contribute to the organization? Finally they developed a business unit strategy--the roadmap for achieving their mission.

1. Mission/ Strategy

Unit Mission

Our unit exists to serve our retail customers and consumers:

- To effectively sell and service the total beverage portfolio, providing a single point of contact for customer enquiries, and the prompt resolution of issues.
- To effectively serve our retail customers, we must also serve our internal customers. We must understand their requirements and deliver excellent service.
- We must also build shareholder value by controlling costs, improving productivity and continuing to grow professionally.

Business Unit Strategy

To drive profitable volume growth by shifting from a field sales structure to a centralized telephone sales structure:

- Focus on customers and consumers
- Strengthen our competitive position
- Enable sales force to concentrate on outlet development rather than order generation
- Drive efficiency

Here is how the CSC team created a customer map. In addition to their final retail customers, they also serve four internal customers: Key Accounts, Future Consumption, Immediate Consumption, and Distribution.

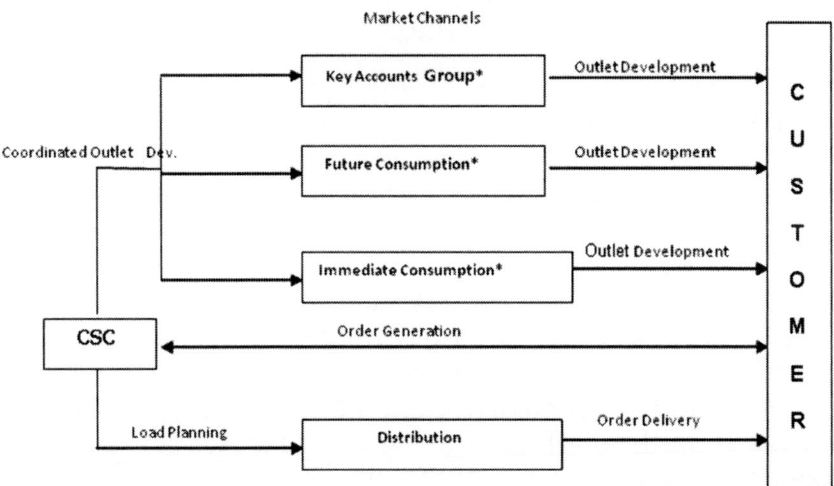

* Key Account Group: major supermarkets, restaurant chains, etc.
Future Consumption: independent grocers, Mom and Pops, etc.
Immediate Consumption: pubs, restaurants, convenience stores, etc.

Key Indicators

Next they translated the strategy into actionable key indicators. The CSC team concentrated on three key result areas: functional productivity, customer satisfaction, and strategy execution. Both team and individual key indicators were identified.

2. Key Indicators

Functional Indicators:
• Quarterly sales targets by tell-sales agent and by channel
• Calls per day-90-100
• Strike rate(ratio of orders to calls)
• Full goods returned due to incorrect order taking/invoicing
• Volume Generating Activities:
  o Product distribution/SKUs
  o New products/packs introduced/resale
  o Promotions booked

Customer Satisfaction Indicators: • Timely resolution of customer enquires • Retail Customer Satisfaction Surveys- 2 times a year • Internal Customers Satisfaction Surveys—benchmark annually
Execution Indicators: • On-Job Coaching—actual Vs monthly plan • Sit-in and evaluate review meetings with standards checklist

If we compare the key indicators with the strategy, we see they are well aligned. The right things are being measured. Functional indicators measure volume, volume-generating activities and productivity. Customer Satisfaction indicators measure both internal and final customer satisfaction. Execution indicators measured the effectiveness of on-job coaching and review meetings. These indicators include both hard quantifiable measures, and soft qualitative measures. They also did a good job of getting the measures down to the "sharp end"--to the agent level where the real work occurs.

Tracking

An effective tracking system provides accurate and timely information on actual performance versus target. Initially the CSC team could only get weekly performance data by telephone agent. They felt they needed daily performance data by agent to quickly solve problems and to stay on track. The Information Technology (IT) group responsible for developing the tracking system disagreed. They felt the current program was fine and changes would be costly. The general manager of the operation finally had to settle the issue. His conclusion was:

> ***"If the CSC team needs this information to manage the performance of their group and improve our efficiency and customer service then that is what we need to do. That is why we created the group. Let's find a cost-effective way to make it happen."***

Each unit has to decide what kind of information it needs to manage its own performance, and then be willing to fight for it. As you can see below, the CSC team used both state of the art software as well as manual tracking with display boards. Tracking was transparent to both the team and to the next level of management.

3. Tracking
• Margin Minder software--sales by outlet by agent • Promotions booked, new product intro., etc.–manual tracking posted on display board • CRM software-provides sales history by customer for pre-call planning • CTI software-links call-ins to CRM to deal with enquires

On-Job Coaching

The CSC team had both a training program supported by the HR group that focused on planned development, and an on-job coaching program that dealt with real-time performance problems. When a performance problem surfaced in a weekly review meeting and it was caused by a skill deficiency, on-job coaching was planned for the next week. Performance improvements were expected the following week and were monitored at the review meeting. This was called coaching-against-a-variance.

4. Coaching
• Current skills of agents were assessed with skills matrix and plans developed. • Supervisors conduct on-job coaching–3 coaching sessions per agent per qtr. • Coaching-against-a-variance as required. • Regular monitoring of telephone sales calls versus call standards. • Sales scripts for new products and promotions.

Review

Performance review meetings involved regular face-to-face monitoring of actual performance versus target, rewarding positive performance, analyzing variances, and taking action.

5. Review
• Daily key indicator results by agent posted on display board. • Weekly team meetings to review weekly targets by agent. • Internal customers (Key Account Mgr, Future Consumption Mgr, Immediate Consumption Mgr, and Distribution Supervisor) attend meeting to monitor service level agreements and to plan coordinated outlet development. • Performance variances caused by a skill-deficiency become part of on-job coaching plan for next week. • Performance related bonuses (30% of fixed salary)

The CSC team posted volume, volume-generating activities, and productivity key indicators daily by agent in rank order.

Public posting of performance in rank order can be intimidating in the wrong hands. It worked well with the CSC team. Their rigorous on-job coaching program quickly corrected performance variances. Also, internal customers attended the weekly reviews. Service level agreements and customer satisfaction measures were reviewed, problems were solved, and plans for the future were discussed. This helped keep the boundaries open between functions and levels. A one page summary of the CSC system can be found in the appendix.

Great Systems Create Great Teams

The CSC unit built a great system and a great team. All five components of the system worked in harmony. As a result the planning and execution were well aligned, and the organization was considered a model for the industry.

"A team is a small number of people with complementary skills who are committed to a common purpose, performance goals, and approach for which they hold themselves mutually accountable." [2]

The healthiest aspect of the CSC team was that both individually and collectively they held themselves accountable. If they fell below target on a key indicator, it triggered a collaborative effort to "find a way to get back on target." They owned the system, and it seemed to operate effectively even when the team leader was absent - a great example of a simple disciplined system. The system was mandated from top, but built from the ground up.

Fits and Finishes

Our five-component system has proven effective in the fast-moving-consumer-goods (FMCG) industry. We believe it has application in other industries with some modifications. All organizations, after all, need to manage performance. And all need a clear strategy, performance indicators, information systems, coaching and performance review.

The system, however, needs to fit the specific needs of the business. Systems can vary depending on factors like:

- Strategic focus
- Size of the organization
- Complexity and variability of the task
- Readiness of the team
- Loose-tight control

Based on these and other factors, the system may need to be modified in terms of the number and type of performance indicators, performance standards, performance period (days, weeks, months) and the frequency of review. For example, a pharmaceutical R&D group which is involved in innovation and creative science is likely to have a looser system overall than a computer chip manufacturer, which is engaged in precision production.

Chapter Summary

The system is the great flywheel of execution. The best systems are simple in design and disciplined in application.

System: Keys to Execution

- They have five components working together like the fingers of a hand.

- They are guided by the five attributes of an effective system.

- They avoid the four common systems problems.

As good as any system can be, it is never a finished product. Like a high performance engine, it requires regular maintenance. Key indicators need to be continuously realigned with changes of the strategy; performance tracking needs to become faster and simpler; review meetings need to become shorter and sharper.

Chapters 6-10 focus on each of the five components of the system. They include best practices, survey data, and a structure approach for developing each component.

Part 2: Designing the Performance Management System

Chapters 6-10 examine the five components of the system in detail. Best practices are shared, and a guided process for aligning each component is provided. Several approaches to implementing an organizational change agenda are discussed in chapter 11.

Chapter 6
Strategic Planning

In a global economy, the execution guides the plan just as often as the plan guides the execution.

Strategic planning identifies the best competitive fit for a company based on its strengths and the opportunities that exist or emerge in the business environment.

As the global economy spins ever faster, it generates major problems and major opportunities. Strategic planning has become a full-time job requiring continuous surveillance of the environment and continuous collaboration of those that plan and execute the strategy.

The strategic plan functions in three ways. First and foremost, it sets the overall direction of the business. Second, it sets the direction for the performance management system, providing a vector for aligning key indicators, tracking, and performance reviews with the strategy. Third it serves as a benchmark for assessing the alignment of the organization. Once the strategy is clearly defined, the next step in the planning process is to determine if the current organization can in fact execute the strategy. If not, one or both need to realigned.

In the past, the strategic plan was the bible that guided execution. Managers were taught to plan their work, and then to work their plan. In a fast-moving global economy however, execution often guides the plan. Evidence of this is seen in the profusion of "what-if contingencies" calling for more "if-then scenarios." It is often better to engage first and then to plan. As a consequence, field managers need to be more involved in shaping the plan as they execute it.

> ***The Conductor and the Quarterback***
>
> In stable times, executing the plan is like conducting a symphony orchestra. Every note of the composition has been scripted. No improvisation is required or welcomed. It is the conductor's job to ensure that every musician precisely executes the plan.
>
> In an environment of constant change, planning and execution overlap. An NFL coach and their quarterback (QB) spend hours studying the film of their next opponent: analyzing the Xs and Os, detecting tendencies, and identifying opportunities. The game plan is created from this analysis: schemes, match-ups, and new plays. At kickoff the game plan is in the coach's hand and taped to the QB's arm. When the offense takes the field, the QB huddles the team, calls the play, steps to the line of scrimmage, surveys the defense, and if needed calls an audible. From this point on, the QB receives an endless stream of feedback which shapes his play calling---from the last play run, from teammates on the field, from the coach on the sidelines. A lot of strategic learning and planning occurs on the field.

An NFL quarterback is at the center of an amazing decision-making system...an open system that is both fast and flexible. The quarterback executes according to plan on one play, and improvises at the last second on the next.

One of the distinctive features of COBRA is the "Red Box in the Middle," a tool designed to push responsibility for planning and operational decision-making as close as possible to the market. It is similar to the system that supports an NFL quarterback, because it is the synthesizing point for executing the game plan and responding to a changing environment. We will cover the red box shortly. In the meantime, just keep in mind that COBRA has a fully integrated view of planning strategy and bringing it to life in a competitive marketplace.

Today's planning process is certainly less tidy and straight-forward than in the past - but no less important. Strategic planning is still the core process for establishing the direction of the business, for providing the roadmap for achieving the corporate vision.

COBRA aligns strategy with execution through a process that involves four steps, illustrated in chart 1. It combines a step by step process and continuous-loop learning. The rest of this chapter examines these four steps in detail.

- Assessing the Business Environment
- Aligning the Strategy with the Environment
- Aligning the Organization with the Strategy
- Streamlining the Execution of the Strategy

Chart 1

The COBRA Alignment Process

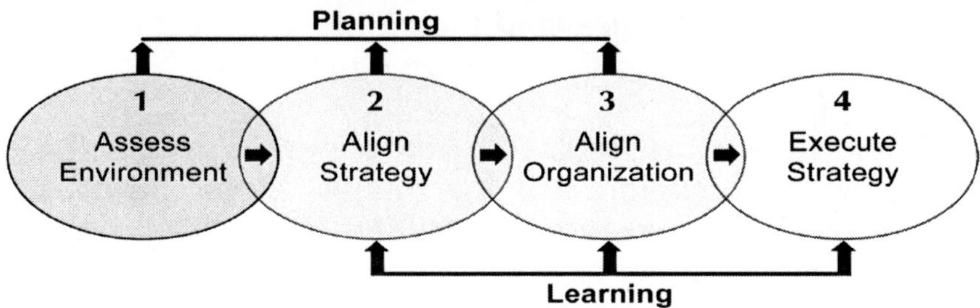

1. Assessing the Business Environment

In assessing the environment, planners must understand both the factors that help the team prepare to plan and the Five Drivers of Change.

Preparing to Plan: Forming the Planning Team

In large organizations it is easy to separate the planners from those who execute the plan. To facilitate input from both, a collaborative planning and decision making process is needed. In preparing to plan the following issues need to be determined:

- Composition of the planning team (head office, business units, field mgrs., etc.)
- Role of each team member
- Plans and decisions to be made centrally
- Plans and decisions to be made locally
- The process for revising and modifying plans

Preparing to Plan: The Company Vision

A company's vision is its North Star that guides strategic planning and decision making. Another way to think of vision is that it is the way the company defines success. Vision is important in determining those opportunities that will be pursued and those that will be avoided. Without a clear corporate vision, major mistakes can be made.

> ***"The most common error in strategic management is setting a detail-oriented strategic process in motion before top management has articulated its vision. Without a vision to drive the strategic process, the energies in each subsequent step will diverge—and the ultimate impact of strategic decisions will be undermined."*** [1]

A vision statement should be broad enough to challenge management to explore new markets as things change, yet not so broad that it takes them away from their core principles and competencies. For example, Intel's corporate vision is to 'do a great job for our customers, employees and stockholders by being the preeminent building block supplier to the worldwide Internet economy'.[2] The company's vision could be too limiting if Intel only wanted to be the preeminent builder of microchips. It could be too broad, if the goal was to be the preeminent company in the worldwide internet economy. This broader vision might lead Intel into markets beyond its core competency.

Sometimes the decisive impact of a company's vision is clear for all to see. Not long ago the European airline Easy-Jet applied its vision to avoid straying from its area of competence.

> Easy-Jet, Europe's second-largest budget carrier, has no intention of seeking a joint venture to take advantage of the open-skies agreement on trans-Atlantic airline services, says its founder, Stelios Haji-Ioannou.
>
> "Easy-Jet, Europe's second-largest budget carrier, will not deviate from its current business model of short flights, one class, all economy."
>
> The announcement last week that Air-France - KLM Group and Delta Air Lines Inc. planned a joint venture to share profits and revenue on trans-Atlantic routes led analysts to suggest that wider combinations in the industry could be on the way.[3]

The corporate vision serves as the over-arching statement of purpose and direction for a company. Strategic plans explore ways to achieve the vision.

Preparing to Plan: Planning Styles

In preparing to plan, it is important to keep in mind that various planning and problem-solving styles can be employed. The model illustrated in Chart 2 is adapted from Henry Mintzberg's Managerial Style Triangle.[4] A combination of all three styles is often needed in developing strategic plans or solving complex problems.

Chart 2

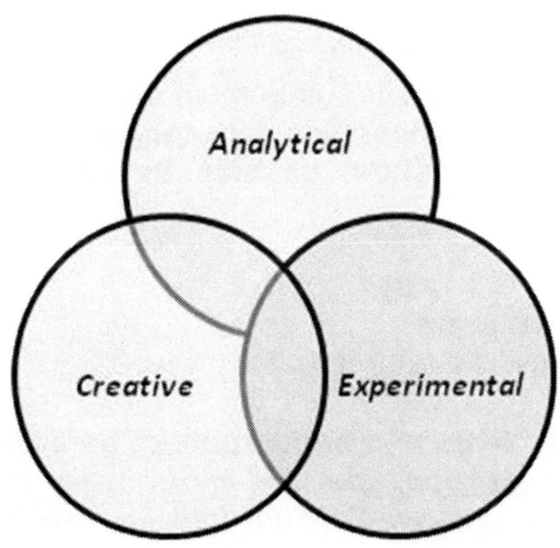

Analytical Style: Staying Inside the Box

This style seeks a solution through reasoning, sound logic, rigorous examination of the facts and following the numbers. Its main characteristics are:

- Logical, relies on scientific analysis and factual information
- Linear, one item of knowledge leads to another
- Convergent, separates essentials from mass of information
- Deductive, makes inferences from available data

Creative Style: Moving Outside the Box

This style is ideal for developing a plan or solving a problem that requires a fresh approach. An organization can be blinded to new ideas by assumptions and practices that creep into its culture. Creative planning starts with the solution, a vision of the future, and then works backward to achieve it. Its main characteristics are:

- Non-logical
- Lateral, going outside the 'obvious' line of thought
- Divergent, expands the problem and areas for solution
- Intuitive, jumps to conclusions without proof

Experimental Style: Engaging to Plan

When there is no obvious solution, an organization often can learn more by experimentation. This can also take some of the risk out of a "bet the farm" decision. Its main characteristics are:

- Ready - Fire - Aim
- Trial and Error
- Test possible options, pilot projects

"Visionary companies make some of their best moves by experimentation, trial and error, opportunism, and quite literally-accident. What looks in retrospect like

brilliant foresight and preplanning was often the result of 'Let's just try a lot of stuff and keep what works'." [5]

In the following example a beverage sales team moves from an analytical style which wasn't working to an experimental style. The team wanted to determine the optimum call frequency (in terms of cost, volume growth and customer satisfaction) for sales developers who called on the grocery and convenience store channel. Should it be biweekly, weekly, or fortnightly?

They first analyzed their sales records, seeking to understand the historical relationship between sales volume and call frequency. This was a logical inquiry; however the number of SKUs had dramatically increased in recent years so the data was less relevant. They then turned to industry standards related to sales force effectiveness, and various software modeling programs. Again they were unable to find any clear cut answers.

Finally they tried an experimental approach. They identified three sales areas within the channel that had the same distribution of outlets. One sales developer called on the outlets in his area on a biweekly basis, another called on his outlets on a weekly basis, and the third called on his outlets on a fortnightly basis. The study was conducted for a month. Cost of sales, volume growth, and customer satisfaction were tracked in all three areas. Once the data was in--and it was timely and relevant--the team returned to an analytical style to determine the optimum call frequency.

They found that a biweekly call was too often. The new product introductions, promotions, and merchandising done on the first call of the week needed little addition attention. There wasn't much to do. The fortnightly call was found to be not often enough. The merchandising was in poor shape, the competition had encroached on shelf space, and sales volume lagged compared to the rep making weekly calls. So the sales team determined that a weekly call was optimum from the stand point of cost, volume, and customer satisfaction.

In planning and problem solving, it is important to be conscious of both the process and the outcome. If the outcome is not satisfactory, you can change the process by shifting planning styles. The simple message: don't get stuck in one style.

Five Change-Drivers

Changes to the business environment are usually led by five change-drivers illustrated in chart 3.[6] They provide an effective way of assessing the business environment. The examples below reflect the fast-moving consumer goods industry.

Five Change-Drivers	
Consumer-led Drivers	• Changes in lifestyle—health, fitness • Both parents working • Changes in disposable income • Demand for convenience
Technology-led Drivers	• Information Technology • Manufacturing technology • Reengineering Processes • On-line customer service
Capital-led Drivers	• Interest rates/cost of money • Ability to sell stock to raise capital • Debt
Government-led Drivers	• Federal and state Laws • Environmental Issues—EPA • Occupational Health and Safety—OSHA • EU Regulations
Competitor-led Drivers	• New competitive products and pricing • Price discounting by competitors • Consolidation of competitors

Technological-led drivers, for example, have a major impact on how companies go to market. McDonalds and Papa John's distribute mobile coupons on cell phones - take your cell phone to the restaurant and redeem. Some consumers shop for the best gas price by entering an area code on their cell phone. I-Pods have changed the methods of purchasing and listening to music.

2. Aligning the Strategy with the Business Environment

Now we move to the second step of strategic planning. After the planning team has completed an environmental assessment, it will have an understanding of the current realties, both the problems and the opportunities. Now the team is ready to develop plans to align strategy with the environment.

Five planning models are discussed in this section. The first two models, Structural Tension and Decision Scenarios, employ all three planning styles discussed earlier, but they rely most heavily on the creative style. The final three include: an industry analysis model, a market execution model, and a channel analysis model. They rely more on an analytical style.

Planning Model: Structural Tension

With this creative approach, you start with the solution, your vision of how you want it to be, and then create a plan to get there. Conversely with an analytical approach you start by defining the problem and then seek to understand the cause of the problem and develop an action plan. Structural tension helps a team break free from simply tinkering with the existing situation. It encourages striking out in a new direction.

> ***"Fixing something that is ill-designed to begin with does little to help us achieve our aims...fixing something means that we take what is there and repair it. Redesigning something means that we start from scratch and rethink the basic premise that guides us."*** [7]

Structural tension is illustrated in chart 4. The starting point is the vision. From there the next step is to assess the current reality to identify what is standing in the way of the vision. Dissonance between the vision and the current reality creates structural tension. The tension operates on both a conscious and an unconscious level to generate an action plan to achieve the vision. It stimulates both urgency for change and a search for a solution.

Chart 4

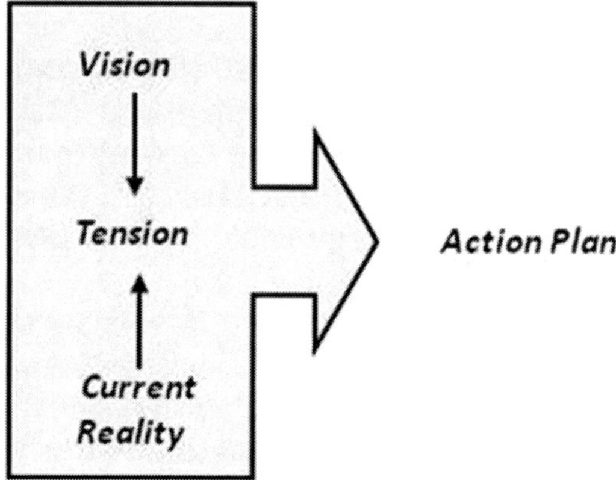

Chart 5 illustrates how structural tension is applied in a specific case – the redesign of an ineffective sales function. In this scenario, defining current reality involved an assessment of the current structure, system and culture, as well as economic factors. The action plan was developed by keeping one eye on the vision and one eye on the current reality. There were a variety of action points, some strategic (local market planning), some structural (clarifying roles and pushing decision-making down), some systems (improving performance measurement and conducting regular review meetings), and some cultural (people development and coaching).

Chart 5

Structural Tension: A Case Study

Vision:

Redesign the field sales function to regain leadership in market development, customer satisfaction, and volume growth (indexed against current levels) by 2/2009

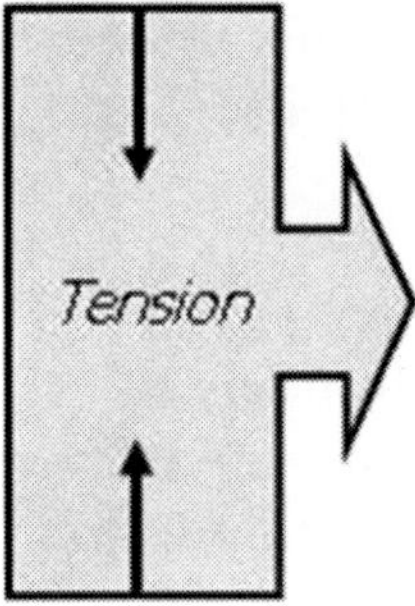

Action Plan

- Local market strategies and plans will be developed as part of the annual strategic planning process.
- Regional and Area managers will have more autonomy developing and executing local market plans.
- They will also be fully accountable for executing plans.
- Measurement system to focus on market execution, on-route coaching, volume growth, and customer satisfaction.
- Regional and Area Managers will spend a major portion of their time in the market coaching and monitoring sales execution.
- Reward system based on volume growth and market execution.
- Regular performance review meetings at all levels to recognize success and quickly resolve performance problems.

****

Monitor progress of this plan quarterly, based on regional targets for volume growth, market execution, and customer satisfaction.

Current Reality

- Economic downturn after 7 years of GNP growth of 6-11%
- Disposable income and consumer spending soared to record levels in that period.
- Lost many of our best people to the booming IT sector.
- Reward system heavily skewed to volume growth Vs. market development.
- Lots of inexperience and complacency; not exploiting local markets.
- Sales management not out in market enough.
- Market became segmented; not exploiting local markets segments.
- Market survey revealed poor execution and customer dissatisfaction.
- Sales volume declined over the last three trimesters.

A fundamental consideration in this case was that economic booms come and go, yet the organization needs to be globally competitive in all seasons. Using the structural tension model, the company envisioned and achieved an effective solution.

Planning Model: Decision Scenarios

When the business environment does not change much, forecasting is a useful planning tool because current trends can be reliably projected into the future. But when the environment is less predictable, it is easy for an organization to get stuck in a "wait and see," reactive mode.

Decision scenarios provide a way to probe the unknown, to anticipate various alternative futures (what ifs?), and to consider possible responses (if-thens).

> ***"Scenarios help managers structure uncertainty when (1) they are based on a sound analysis of reality, and (2) they change the decision makers' assumptions about how the world works and compel them to reorganize their mental model of reality."*** [8]

What if ...

- The price of oil doubles?
- Hurricane insurance increases by 80%?
- Interest rates soar to 12%?
- The FDA doesn't approve your latest wonder drug?
- Sales of a new product exceed projection by 100%?
- Your biggest retail customer introduces a house brand and delists your brand?

If, Then...

Framing a scenario like those above opens up an avenue for the planning team to engage in both rational and creative dialogue. At its best, this model compels the team to come to grips with uncertainty in a disciplined manner:

- Is the above scenario based on a false premise?
- What are your decision making options (If, then)?

- How can you learn more about your options and remove some of the risk?
- How time-sensitive are your options?
- Do you face a "cross-roads decision" you need to make to survive?
- Are there contingencies, short of "betting the farm?"
- Can you delay your decision and let things unfold a bit?
- Can you take an incremental approach?
- How is the rest of the industry likely to respond?

It is also important to identify trigger points for each scenario, as illustrated in chart 6. Trigger points are flashing red lights that indicate it is time to shift from the current plan to the contingency plan.

Chart 6

What If	***Trigger***	***If Then***
If sales exceed forecast by 30% in peak season.	If sales exceed forecast by 25% in first month of peak season and line downtime due to changeovers has increased by 10% of standard.	• Add third shift • Lease temporary warehouse space • Run double loads on direct delivery routes

Planning Model: Five Forces Analysis

Planners often define competition too narrowly, as the rivalry among existing competitors. Michael Porter's classic Five Forces model as seen in chart 7 broadens the competitive arena.

Chart 7

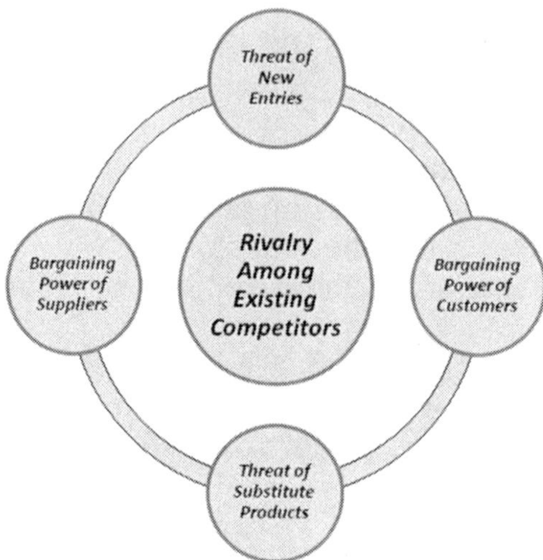

"Competition for profits goes beyond established industry rivals to include four other competitive forces as well: customers, suppliers, potential entrants, and substitute products. The extended rivalry that results from all five forces defines an industry's structure and shapes the nature of competitive interaction within an industry." [9]

Threat of New Entries:

Profitable markets attract new entrants that put pressure on prices, costs, and the rate of investment necessary to compete. An established company can raise the barriers to entrance by understanding what gives it a competitive edge, and continuing to excel in those areas:

- Access to capital
- Distribution system
- Brand equity
- Cost advantage
- Market execution

Bargaining Power of Suppliers:

Powerful supplies can erode your profits by charging higher prices and limiting the quality or service they provide. In selecting suppliers, here are key factors to consider:

- Availability of other suppliers
- Supplier size/concentration
- History of quality/service of suppliers
- Opportunities for long-term partnerships for mutual gain
- Backward integration

Threat of Substitute Products:

Substitutes satisfy your customer's needs by a different means and can be less expensive, more convenient, or higher in quality. This might include: e-mail for express mail, plastic for aluminum, concentrated juice for ready to drink juices. When planning for how to manage substitutes, consider these factors:

- Brand loyalty for your products
- Price elasticity of your products
- Price difference that triggers switching
- Offering products/packages to attract all economic levels (B brands)
- Acquiring substitute products

Bargaining Power of Customers:

Customers apply pressure to gain favorable terms, conditions, and pricing. By demanding a higher level of quality or service, they drive up your costs. In managing customers, these factors are important to consider:

- Size concentration of customers relative to your company
- Dependence on customer as a source of business
- Attractiveness to the customer of substitutes to your product
- Marketing programs that build consumer traffic /profit for your customer

Rivalry among Existing Competitors:

Competitors can intensify the rivalry by: deeper price discounting, new products, ad campaigns, increased service level, etc. In managing competitive rivals, consider the following:

- Number and strength of competitors
- Your share of market and revenue compared to rivals
- Rate of industry growth
- Optimum combination of cost leadership, product differentiation, and segmentation

A beer industry case study in the appendix provides an example of this model.

Planning Model: Four A's of Market Execution

The four A's as illustrated in chart 8 describe what is needed to take a product to market and sell it to the final consumer. It is most relevant to fast moving consumer goods companies that supply the retail trade.

Chart 8

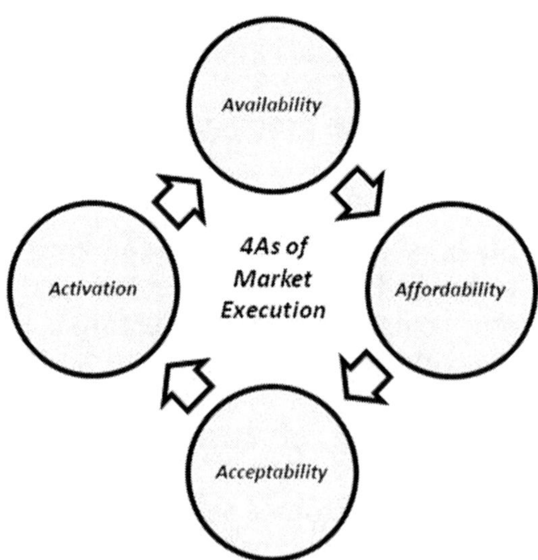

Though the consumer goods company has a major responsibility for executing the 4A's, the retail customer ultimately controls product selection and space allocation. For the consumer goods company, success depends on developing a reliable and supportive partnership with the retailer. Chart 9 is a generic example of the 4 A's from the beverage industry.

Chart 9

Availability	• Provide adequate stock of the appropriate products & packages • Use scan data to manage inventory and space allocation • New account expansion/portfolio selling/category mgmt • Optimize call frequency and order generation to ensure availability
Affordability	• Provide best value proposition to consumer via wholesale pricing • Help retailer identify the best price/value relationship • Provide a portfolio that balances consumer needs and revenue growth • Expand consumer franchise via trial, impulse purchase and brand switching • Use price-elasticity modeling to optimize every-day and promotional pricing • Provide product & packaging options to attract all economic levels
Acceptability	• Provide right products, packages & promotions based on consumer behavior • Create consumer demand by quality advertising • Provide best products and promotions to trigger occasion-based consumers • Deliver quality products and services
Activation	• Stimulate planned and impulse purchase at the point of sale • Execute merchandising standards with space for core and emerging brands • Select high traffic display locations • Establish multiple impulse points/displays • Call to Action: compelling communication (TV ads, pos, billboards, etc)

The 4A's are interdependent and reinforcing. They should be adapted to the needs of the trade channel and the consumer.

The 3A version of this model was developed by The Coca-Cola Company. Mr. Irial Finan, the former CEO of CCHBC, added the 4th A---activation. Irial is one of those rare executives with both a head for the numbers and a passion for execution. The analysis that follows uses this model along with others to analyze a specific channel.

Planning Model: Channel Analysis

An effective channel strategy requires an understanding of what makes a specific channel different from the rest of the market, and how those differences can be exploited. The analysis in chart 10 deals with the grocery channel.

Consider the following as you move through each step of the plan:

- What is going well and needs to continue?
- Where are the problems, gaps and opportunities?
- What are symptoms; what are core causes?
- What needs to change?

Chart 10

Process	*Channel Plan*	*Comments*
1. ***Channel Analysis: 5Ws*** • Who purchases? (demographics) • What? (products/ packages) • Where? (outlet/location in store) • When? (hour/day) • Why? (consumer occasion) [10]	• Brand Plans • Package Plans • Pricing Plans • Merchandising Plans • Picture of Success	This analysis is done for the total market as well as by channel. The Marketing Group does the analysis with input from the Sales Group.
2. ***Industry Analysis*** • Customers • Suppliers • Substitutes • New entrants • Existing Competitors	• Customer Profile • Competitor Profiles	This is done jointly by Marketing and Sales.

3. *Past Performance/ Trends:* • Sales/share Vs. competition • Sales/share by channel • Brand/package by channel • Sales by key customer	• Opportunity Assessment • Channel Sales Objectives • Key Account Objectives	Channel Mgr. and Key Acct. reps. meet with their key customers to identify their needs. This input is factored into the Key Acct. Plans.
4. *Market Execution* • 4A analysis • Promotional execution • Category mgmt. • Cooler/rack penetration	• Promotional Plans • Space Mgmt. Plans • Key Account Plans	These plans are based on historical data and market visits by Mkt. and Sales Mgrs. and retail customers (regional and store mgrs.)
5. *Sales Force Effectiveness* Cobra-Scan assessment of sales mgmt. system and skills assessment(selling & merchandising)	• Modify sales mgmt. system as required • On-job coaching plan	Sales Mgrs. sit-in team leader review meetings to assess key indicators, tracking system, and review. Sales reps are shadowed to assess their current skills and coach as required.

In summary, there are many excellent strategic planning models. The five models we have discussed are representative. At this point, the planning team should have a clear idea of its initial business strategy. Now it's time to determine if the organization can deliver the strategy.

3. Aligning the Organization with the Strategy

Organizational alignment is the third step in the COBRA process. It involves two parts:

- Assessing the Current Alignment
- Developing an Alignment Plan

In stable times, strategy can be executed with relatively minor changes to the organization. Turbulent times however generally call for major realignment of the organization.

Two models for assessing alignment are SWOT Analysis and COBRA-Scan. We will examine how each works based on examples from the beverage industry--an industry that is experiencing tremendous change.

> **Health & Fitness**
>
> In recent years health and fitness have become major concerns for many consumers. Traditional soft drink companies have made a strategic decision to pursue these emerging market segments. Major realignment of the structure, the system and the culture has been needed. This involved developing new competencies in the areas of R&D, marketing, and manufacturing. It also required the redesign of the product development process, restructuring the supply chain and sales function, and articulating the values of health and nutrition to all employees.

SWOT Analysis

SWOT stands for: Strengths, Weaknesses, Opportunities, and Threats. It is a simple, reliable tool to get input from all levels of the organization. It works best as a candid brainstorming session. The categories of Strengths and Weaknesses focus internally on the organization. The categories of Opportunities and Threats focus externally on the environment.

Strengths and Weaknesses (SW)

The analysis can focus on broad organizational issues or on specific functional issues. Chart 11 illustrates a sales forecasting problem spanning several functions. Everyone has something to contribute when discussing the strengths and weaknesses of their function or work group.

Chart 11

Supply Chain		
Strengths	***Weaknesses***	***Realignment Plans***
Enormous growth opportunities in water, juice, health, and energy categories. Responding to consumer trends, a major development of new products and packages in these categories, as well as growth by acquisition.	Major growth in product / package portfolio has overwhelmed the current sales forecasting system. Average Forecast accuracy is 50% causing: • Retail out of stock(OOS) • Excessive stock or OOS in warehouse • Difficult to accurately procure spare parts, raw materials, etc. • Loss in revenues	Develop a consensus-based forecasting process. Forecasting will include input from internal functions and major retail customers: • Identify the best software program to support forecasting process • Clearly define roles and responsibilities of the team • Monitor forecast accuracy-- learn, improve

Chart 12 shows a marketing application related to sales promotion in a retail chain.

Chart 12

Sales / Marketing		
Strengths	***Weaknesses***	***Realignment Plans***
Brand Leader Broad portfolio of products and packages Fair share of shelf space Excellent merchandising at point of sale Good relationship with major chain customers.	Heavy price promotions in large home consumption chains. Fail to optimize promotions: price point, promotional period, incremental sales and revenue.	Identify a revenue mgmt. software package that captures historical data and forecasts results of pricing and promotional plans. Partner with a key chain to track customer purchase behavior (scan data) within chain and jointly plan promotions.

Once the strengths and weaknesses are understood, realignment plans can be developed, as noted in the right hand columns of the two charts above.

SWOT Analysis is an effective planning and problem-solving tool. It is useful in getting issues "on the table" and fostering broad participation from all levels. It lacks, however, a conceptual framework that defines "how things should work." This triggered the development of COBRA-Scan, which identifies key alignment drivers—or "vital signs." They enable you to diagnose alignment issues and prescribe solutions.

COBRA-Scan

As noted in chapter 1, when the organization can't execute the strategy, breakdowns in the structure, the system and the culture—the *Three Points of Pressure*--explain most of the problems most of the time.

COBRA-Scan assesses the key drivers that underpin each of the *Three Points of Pressure* as illustrated in Chart 13.

Chart 13

3 Points of Pressure		
Structure	***System***	***Culture***
Formal Structure	Strategy	Leadership
Boundary Mgmt.	Key Indicators	Vision & Values
Core Processes	Tracking Systems	Norms
Bridging Structure	On-Job Coaching	Core Competencies
	Review	

The scan is normally conducted by a joint client-consultant team. The data gathering takes five to seven days at the pilot location and generally involves:

- Performance Audit for the previous year
- Document Review: strategic plans, key indicators, etc.

- On-Job Observation: actual performance versus standard
- Process Observation: planning, problem solving, and review meetings
- Market Execution: store checks, shadowing field sales, customer interviews
- Leadership Practices: 360˚ peer-based feedback
- Organizational Readiness Survey/Interviews

Some of these methods are standard, while others vary with the specific engagement. The scan starts with a performance audit for the previous year. This identifies positive results as well as major negative variances, which also helps to guide the subsequent data gathering. The following are examples of what we assess.

The System

The system guides the planning and execution of the strategy throughout the organization. We assess strategy and the key indicators at every level and function. The tracking system is assessed by a real-time test of speed, accuracy and relevance. On-job coaching and review meetings are assessed by direct observation versus standard. The scan seeks to answer the following questions:

- Does the system have five integrated components?
- Does it help plan and execute the strategy?
- Is it simple in design?
- Is it disciplined in execution (regular and rigorous coaching and review)?
- Does the system operate across all levels and functions?
- Does it create positive performance pressure?
- Is it optional or mandatory?
- Does it tie rewards to results?
- Our managers at every level held accountable for operating the system?

The Structure

The structure includes both the formal arrangement of functions, levels, and processes and the roles and responsibilities for working within and across these groupings. The scan seeks to answer the following questions:

- Is the formal structure effective (is it aligned with the strategy)?
- Does the structure optimize internal productivity?
- Does the structure optimize customer satisfaction?
- Is the movement of goods and services across functional boundaries effective?
- Has each function defined its customer maps and missions: who they serve and how they interact with other functions?
- Has authority for decision making and problem solving been pushed down to lower levels (point of control)?
- Is there shared accountability for strategic planning and execution?
- Are core business process regularly improved?
- Are bridging structure used to deal with extraordinary issues?

The Culture

Culture, the most elusive of the three points of pressure, deals with the human side of the organization: beliefs, values and competencies of the people. The scan seeks answers to the following questions:

- Is there a vision statement that articulates the company's destination and guiding principles?
- Can the leadership team execute the vision and strategy?
- Are core values understood and modeled by management?
- What aspects of the current culture support the vision and strategy?
- What aspects are dysfunctional and need to be changed?
- Does the training and development process ensure that people have the leadership, management and technical competencies to perform at the highest levels?
- Are managers at every level pro-active in resolving cross-functional and cross-level conflict?

Once the COBRA-Scan is completed and a summary of the findings is prepared, they are shared with managers from all levels and functions of the organization. This is usually done at a one day off-site meeting. The goal is to ensure the scan has correctly uncovered the fundamental issues. The data-sharing also helps build commitment to the change. Some change interventions need to be driven from the top, others involve a more collaborative approach. As much as possible, collaboration works best.

Developing the Final Strategic Plan

The alignment plan is the output of SWOT and COBRA-Scan findings. The planning team now has two important documents to consider: the initial strategic plan and the alignment plan.

Integrating these plans is a lot like a football coach developing a winning game plan, considering the best competitive strategy as well as the team's readiness to execute the plan.

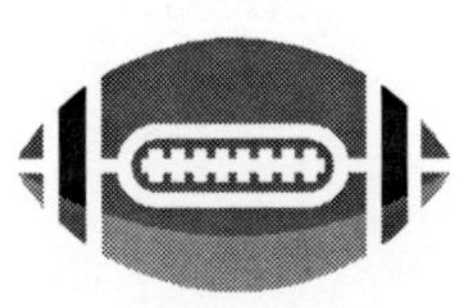

The new offensive strategy has some very exciting strategic options. We also have a lot of rebuilding to do on the offensive side of the line. For now, we need to focus on executing the basics. We will open up the playbook later in the season.

As illustrated in the chart 14, strategic plans identify the objectives and tactics needed to exploit market opportunities, and organizational plans identify the realignment that is needed to execute each strategic objective. Two strategic objectives are discussed in this example.

Chart 14

Initial Strategic Plans		***Organizational Plans***		
Objectives	***Tactics***	***Structure***	***System***	***Culture***
Develop premium priced products for image conscious consumers.	New product definition Product positioning Package profile R & D plan Ad agency plan	Streamline the new product development process	Improve the market execution of sales force. Need clear targets, on-job-coaching, and daily/ weekly reviews at first line sales level.	Currently aligned, continue to build the competency and commitment of the sales force.
Reduce cost per case by 10% across supply chain without sacrificing product or package quality.	Introduce high speed fill technology to all lines Negotiate long term supplier agreements Vertical integration: produce own packaging, etc.	Greatest productivity losses occur at the boundaries between functions. Introduce boundary mgmt. discipline.	Currently aligned	Reduce downtime by training operators on start-up, changeover and sanitation procedures.

Now it is time to determine what is realistic and achievable. In the chart above we can see that some of the organizational factors are currently aligned and others need major realignment. The two plans need to be compared and tested one against the other.

The Final Strategic Plan is the outcome of decisions made in the testing process:

- How much realignment of the organization is needed to execute the strategy?
- How long will it take?
- Is it achievable?
- Can it be accelerated?
- Can we scale back the strategy in the short term while realigning the organization?
- Do we need to pursue both concurrently?

Some strategic plans are beyond the organization's capacity to deliver, in which case it is better to adapt the strategy to the organization, at least in the short term.

"There is a growth rate at which everybody fails and the whole situation results in chaos." [11]

4. Streamlining the Execution of the Strategy

At this point the planning team has reached the fourth and final step of the alignment process. Two approaches to streamlining the execution of strategy will be discussed:

- Aligning the Strategy across Functional Lines
- Red Box in the Middle

Aligning the Strategy across Functional Lines

For many organizations, strategic planning is a two-step process. First the planning team assesses the environment and sets the broad corporate business strategy. Then each function is asked to develop functional strategies to achieve the corporate strategy. These are reviewed and negotiated up and down the line until agreement is reached. Then they are executed. Though there may be some well intentioned discussions about the need for teamwork across functional lines, the focus is primarily on functional productivity.

Chart 15

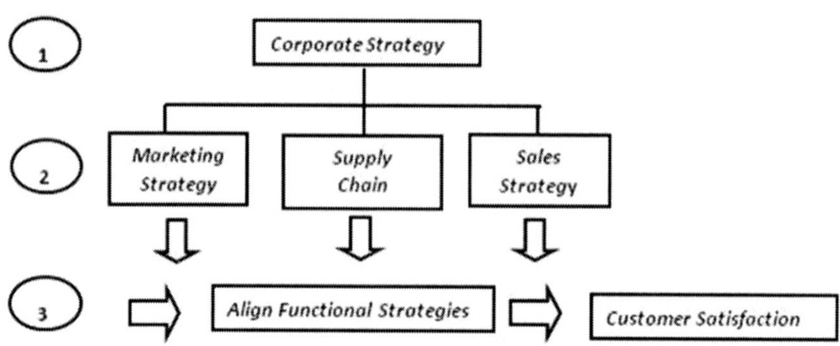

Our most successful clients add a third step to the process - aligning the various functional strategies to optimize both functional productivity and customer satisfaction. Functional alignment greatly reduces disruptive functional boundaries, a major barrier to strategy execution.

Roland and Klaus

They were at it again. The weekly review meeting was never dull, but it was peak season and things weren't going well. Roland, the production manager, was below target on line efficiency and cost per case. Most of his problems were caused by frequent change overs - refitting the line for a different product in the middle of a shift:

"Yes, yes Klaus I've heard it before ... changing consumer tastes, total beverage portfolio, speed to market, more and more new products. Please don't call this a science ... it's more like the lottery. Your sales forecasts are hopeless and the change overs are killing our efficiencies."

Klaus, the marketing manager, was below target on many of the new product introductions:

"My dear Roland, if you can produce it we can sell it. Sales have been great on most new product introductions, consumers like them, retail customers want them, but it's you guys that can't keep up with the demand."

As the Roland-and-Klaus-show ramped up a notch, Dieter, the new general manager, sat quietly in the corner reviewing the strategic plans and objective for the year. Dieter had just come aboard and was trying to get up to speed. Finally, he called time-out:

"Let me see if I understand this. Klaus your strategic plans indicate that you will introduce 25 new brands and packages this year. Is that correct? (Klaus nods) Ok fine, and Roland won't that require a lot more start-up and change over time? (Roland nods). Now Roland I know you want to find ways to improve your efficiencies every year, as you should. But if nothing else changes, and you have 25 new products coming on stream, with the additional start-up and change over time, your efficiencies have got to go down. I'd like you to set a realistic target for yourself... and if needed, bring on a few more people to help with changeovers. The lost revenue from out of stocks far outweighs the additional labor costs. And Klaus I want to start sitting in your weekly sales forecasting meeting. Let's see if we can find a way to improve the sales forecasts."

This sounds like a typical, day-to-day, operational problem. Like many such problems however, it is rooted in the strategic planning process. In this example, Dieter went on to introduce functional alignment to the strategic planning process, and thereby streamlined the execution of strategy.

Red Box in the Middle

When the Red Box is located midway between the head office and the front lines, the responsibility for planning and decision-making moves closer to the market. The planning guides the execution, and the execution guides the planning. This is illustrated chart 16.

Chart 16

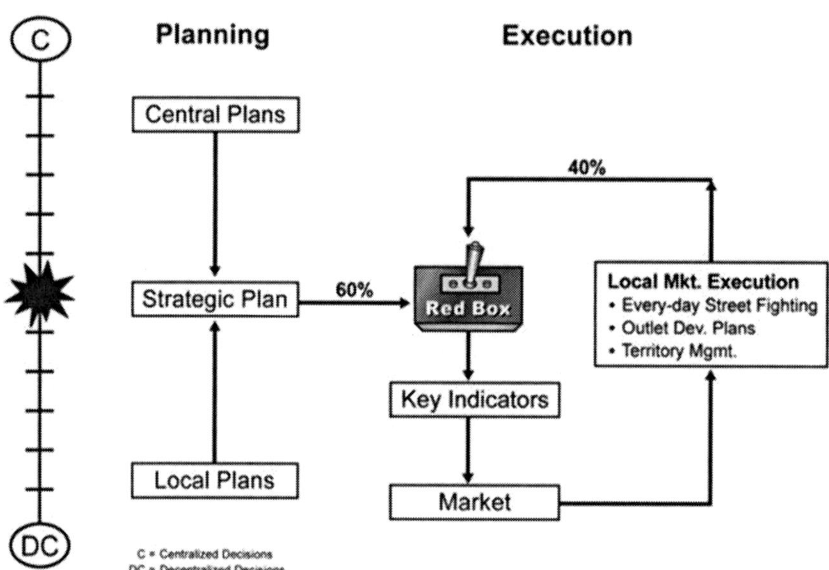

Aligning the planning and decision making with a dynamic market is a challenge even with a single-tier business. It becomes a far bigger challenge with a multi-tiered business serving global, national, and highly diverse local markets. In the beverage industry this usually involves a three-tier structure: franchisor, franchisee, and retail customer. All are directly or indirectly serving the consumer.

Planning

On the left side of chart 16 is the formal planning process in which the central strategy group works cooperatively with the market execution group. In dynamic markets, sixty to seventy percent of the plans that get executed are determined in the formal planning process.

The head office sets the broad sales, share and revenue growth objectives. Then the regional sales groups develop specific regional strategies. Key customers provide input as well. The regional strategies are designed to exploit local market opportunities while falling within the broad strategic guidelines of the company. As noted earlier, strategic plans should be parked in the regions, not at the head office.

Execution

Local market execution, illustrated on the right side of chart 16, is a line-of-sight, outlet-by-outlet discipline. It is driven by a commitment to customer service and operational excellence. Passion, as much as process, drives execution. The following approaches are characteristic:

- *Every-Day Street Fighting* - an immediate response to a local market problem or opportunity. This involves executing the merchandising standards and the 4A's on an every-call basis - exploit/fix now, or exploit/fix next call tactics.

- *Outlet Development Plans* - a focus on high potential outlets that require major development over a period of time to optimize.

- *Territory Management* - giving authority to local managers to run their territory as an independent business.

When each of these approaches is fully functioning in an organization, 30-40 percent of plans that are executed will be based on what has been learned from the market *after* the formal planning process is finalized. This may include: exploiting an unanticipated opportunity, correcting a merchandising problem, fulfilling a retail customer request, responding to a competitive threat, and so on.

This leads to a key point - there will never be enough focus groups and concept tests to figure out exactly what the consumer or the retailer really wants. The marketplace, not market research, ultimately determines if strategy is on target.

Field sales operations that are good at local market execution are held responsible for both sales volume and volume-generating activities. Sales volume is a "hard number" - relatively easy to quantify and monitor. Volume-generating activities include the merchandising standards discussed earlier in the 4A's model. Most are "soft-numbers" that are harder to quantify and monitor.

Store checks are the best way to monitor the soft numbers—to go and see. The store check report illustrated in chart 17 is a summary of checks conducted by a sales supervisor and the sales representative that calls on these stores.

Chart 17

Store Check Report			
Store	***Merchandising Standards****	***Action Points***	***Follow-up***
Independent Super #278	80%	Main display excellent, space allocation good; need more permanent secondary displays. Sell in juice display near fresh fruit area and water display near health foods area.	To be installed by next Friday, bring pictures to review meeting.
Shell Station #306	75%	Candy and ice cream displays dominate the main counter. Sell benefits and profits of our product and gain at least equal display space.	By tomorrow, call me when complete.

3 small grocery stores with common owner	59%	Store checks of all three outlets reveal that main display area for our products is too late in shopping pattern. Prepare presentation for owner based on historical sales and testimonials from similar outlets with display earlier in shopping pattern.	We will rehearse sales presentation on Monday am and arrange a sales call to owner on Monday pm.
New health food store under construction		Meet with store manager with a total design for the store and grand opening rally and promotion by 15th of month.	Meet with key accounts group and develop total design. Set meeting with store manager within ten days. Internal review of design by 12th of month.
Mom & Pop Grocery #21	30%	This was a great outlet for us. It is in terrible shape. We went to sleep and the competition has moved in. This will take several months of hard work to get right. Need an Outlet Development Plan with key steps and a timetable.	Develop plan and review internally next week. Meet with dealer, gain approval and begin implementation by 15th of month. Monitor progress in weekly review meeting.
* % based on store check with merchandising standards checklist			

Some of the action points noted in the report need to be done in addition to the formal plan. Some have an even higher priority than the plan and should be done first. Others should be done instead of what was planned.

At this point nothing has gone wrong. The formal planning was developed with the collaborative input of all parties. The field sales team is committed to executing the plan and responding to local market opportunities. The sales supervisor is out in the market observing the execution and solving problems--so far, so good.

This illustrates the central role of the *Red Box in the Middle*, synthesizing input from the formal plan and from the marketplace and making the best decisions in a timely way.

Now if the Red Box were located at the head office, there would be no orderly process to realign the formal plan with emerging local opportunities. The strategy would become "frozen" in execution, and an imperfect plan would be executed. Or, middle managers feeling the heat from both the head office and the field might ask the field sales team to execute both the formal plan and plans emerging from the local market--a sure fire way to burn-out the sales team.

Conversely, if the red box were too decentralized things could go wrong as well. With too much local autonomy, programs and promotions with market-wide application would not be uniformly executed across the total market.

> ***"If left alone field people will tend to react to what the competition and the retailers are doing and have a lot less sensitivity to what is going on with the consumer."***
>
> Jim Stuart, former Marketing Director,
> Consolidated Coca-Cola Bottlers [12]

As command-central for planning and decision-making, the Red Box is ideally situated in the middle. In that position it facilitates a continuous loop of informed and insightful decision making between the central planning group and the local market execution group.

Building the Red Box

The system, the structure, and the culture provide the "architectural bones" of the Red Box. The following is an example of how the red box was built between the sales and marketing functions in a highly successful bottling operation.

The System:

Both functions needed to ensure that the performance management system operated within and across their functions.

The Structure:

Several structural changes were made:

- Boundary Management: Roles and responsibilities needed to be redefined so that all those involved in strategic planning and execution -Trade Marketing, Key Accounts, and Field Sales – were jointly responsible for results. This discouraged planners from blaming executors when results were poor. All parties had responsibility for solving problems, whether this required a change of plans, improving the execution, or both.

- Process Improvement: The strategic planning process had to incorporate timely input and decision making from all levels and in some areas from several tiers.

- Bridging Structure: Each field sales region appointed a manager to be a liaison between the central planning group and the field sales group. Liaison managers reported directly to the VPs of Regional Sales and had a dotted line responsibility to the central planning group. They also had veto power over plans that didn't meet the needs of the local field sales group, as long as they fell within the broad strategic guidelines.

The Culture:

- Values: The values of customer service, teamwork and market execution were articulated and practiced by all levels and functions.

- Competence: Since field managers and supervisors were more involved in the planning and problems solving, they needed to be trained for these tasks.

The *Red Box in the Middle* is a valuable tool for pushing responsibility for planning and operational decision-making as close as possible to the market. The resulting advantages are speed, flexibility and superior market execution.

Chapter Summary

Steps 1-3 of the COBRA Alignment Process illustrated in chart 18 guide the planning of the strategy, and the assessment of the organization's ability to execute the strategy. The final strategic plan incorporates both the business objectives and the organizational alignment plan (the change agenda). It sets forth what can realistically be executed.

In step 4 both the business objectives and the change agenda are executed. Functional alignment and the *Red Box in the Middle* are two excellent ways to streamline the execution.

Chart 18

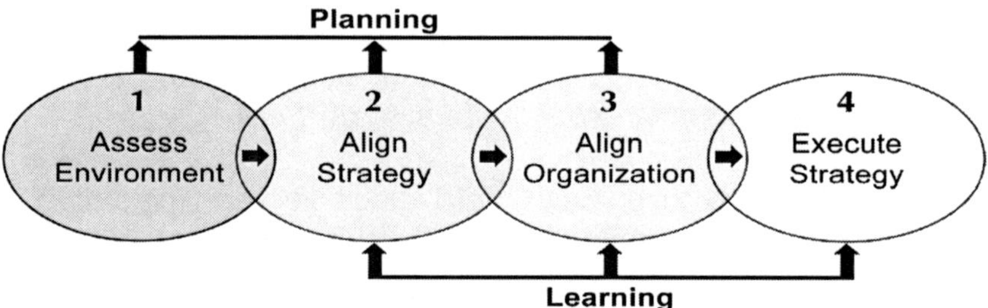

In the next chapter we focus on identifying key indicators and aligning them with the strategy. It includes best practices, survey data, and a structured process for identifying key indicators. Then the remaining chapters focus on tracking key indicators, on-job coaching, and performance review, rounding out the performance management system.

Chapter 7
Key Indicators

Bully-Metrics: Hard numbers from the top tend to push out soft numbers from the bottom.

Key indicators translate strategic objectives into measurable performance. They enable managers to plan work, set targets, and monitor results.

There is nothing new about using key indicators to monitor progress. Someone was out there counting stones when the Great Wall of China was built in 206 BC. One of the most widely used tools in business today is Management by Objectives (MBO), which converts broad objectives into specific key indicators down functional lines.

Key indicators link the strategic plan and the execution of the plan, and need to be responsive to both. While they are indispensable, they also present certain challenges. An aggregate indicator like return on investment provides a critical bottom-line measure, but can obscure a partial indicator that may be creating a poor return. Just as a partial indicator like on-time delivery provides information on only one dimension of customer service.

Key indicators are a useful abstraction, one step removed from reality. At their best they indicate, they provide a red flag, an alarm bell--an early warning system. They keep us on track and prompt us to take a closer look when a variance occurs. This chapter will discuss:

1. Five Best Practices

2. Three Types of Key Indicators
3. The Key Indictor Worksheet
4. Risk/Readiness Matrix

****

1. Five Best Practice

We have designed some of these practices; others have been borrowed from our most successful clients. Some are timeless fundamentals; others were created to deal with the unique challenges of our time.

 Key Indicators are Aligned

The best companies translate broad strategic objectives into actionable key indicators, and identify the individual or team that is responsible. All three need to be aligned.

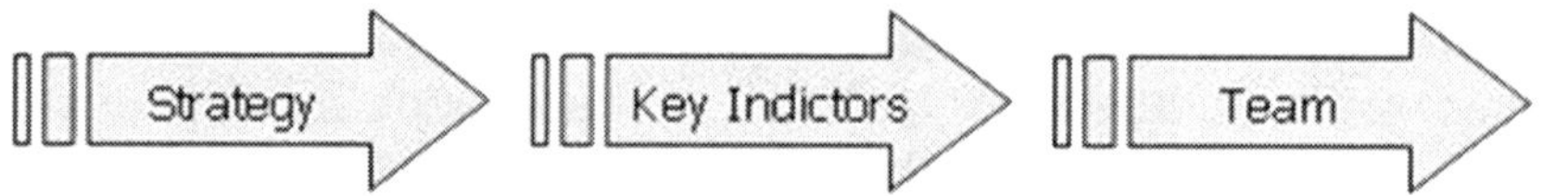

In stable times, strategy and key indicators don't change much from year to year, so alignment is usually not a big deal. You develop your plans and indicators, and then you get on with the business of executing them. In turbulent times, however, alignment is an on-going process of adapting your strategy and key indicators to an ever-changing business environment.

The most common alignment problems occur when key indicators do not exist for a strategic objective, as below, or when the current key indictors do not accurately measure the strategic objective. In this example, the following strategic objective was prominently displayed on the company's boardroom wall.

We will provide products and services which consistently meet or exceed customer standards at the lowest cost.

This strategy was certainly aligned with the market. If well executed, it would provide a major competitive advantage. We observed, however, that no key indicators had been identified to monitor the objective. There was no way of translating intent into action. We recommended the following:

- Define customer service standards with the input of customers
- Identify key indicators to measure the delivery of customer standards (and your competitors)
- Identify key indicators to measure cost of goods (and your competitors)
- Clarify responsibility for key indicators.
- Use the performance management system to monitor and manage the strategy.

Now let's look at some examples of how alignment is achieved. Chart 1 illustrates how a sales unit tested the alignment of its key indicators with its strategic objectives.

Chart 1

	Strategic Objectives			
	1. Cost Control Profit	***2. Sales Volume***	***3. Volume-Generating Activities***	***4. People Development/ Execution***
KEY INDICATORS	• OPEX per case • Margin contribution • Sales Depot P&L • Credit Days • Cost of Sales • Cooler Profitability • Etc.	• Volume & Share by Region • Volume by Channel • Vending volume • Tel-Sell Volume • Key account Volume • Etc.	• Net Numeric Distribution • New Accounts • Promotional Lift • Forward Stock • Out of Stock • Merchandising Standards • Etc.	• Coach Review meetings • On-route coaching • Competency certification • Job Rotation/ Cross-training • Etc.

Once sales objectives were clearly defined, the following questions were posed: What is the best way to measure our objectives? Are we currently measuring the right things? Is there a faster, simpler, or better way to do this? This was an early draft but it illustrates the testing process.

This approach helped identify the most meaningful key indicators for each strategic objective. Later the sales team went on to align these indicators by sub-unit and level (see chart 9).

Chart 2 illustrates how a production unit tested the alignment of key indicators up and down the three levels of its function. The unit also determined when key indicators would be monitored and reviewed using the following format:

Chart 2

Production Key Indicators			
1. Who (responsibility)	***2. What (key Indicators)***	***3. When***	
		Monitor	***Review***
General Mgr & Technical Mgr	1. system line efficiency 2. GMP--good manufacturing practices, an internal audit of quality system requirements 3. concentrate yields 4. cost per unit case 5. cases per man hour	Daily	Monthly
Production Mgr & 15 Shift Supervisors	1. system line efficiency 2. GMP 3. concentrate yields 4.cost per unit case 5. case per man hour	Daily	Weekly
Shift Supervisors & Team	1. system line efficiency 2. GMP 3. concentrate yields	Continuously	End of shift

- *Who*: the level, sub-unit, or individual responsible for the key indicator.
- *What*: the key indicators for each level. Some are common to all levels, and others are unique to a level. The first

three key indicators for all levels are common, though the scope and frequency of review vary by level.

- *When*: how often key indicators are checked. This includes both the continuous monitoring of progress by the responsible manager, supervisor, or individual and the periodic team review of results.

This operation had five production lines each running three shifts a day. The 15 shift supervisors monitor three key indicators continually throughout the shift, and conduct a team review at the end of the shift. The review takes no more than five minutes. At the next level up, the production manager has five key indicators which he monitors daily and reviews weekly with all of the shift supervisors, and so on.

In these two examples, key indicators are *vertically aligned* up and down functional lines. Each level and sub-unit is measuring the right things. There is agreement on who, what, and when. Later in this chapter we will discuss the alignment of customer satisfaction indicators across the organization, or *horizontal alignment*. You need both to optimize performance

Key Indicators are Hard and Soft

All businesses have their hard and soft sides as illustrated in chart 3. Hard indicators are quantifiable results that can be expressed as a number on a spread sheet—sales volume, cost, profit. Soft indicators include things like: customer satisfaction, quality, and market execution. They are certainly *key* indicators--capturing critical moments of truth-- but to track them generally requires direct observation of behavior on the job. Both types are important, both need to be measured and managed. The best companies do both.

Chart 3

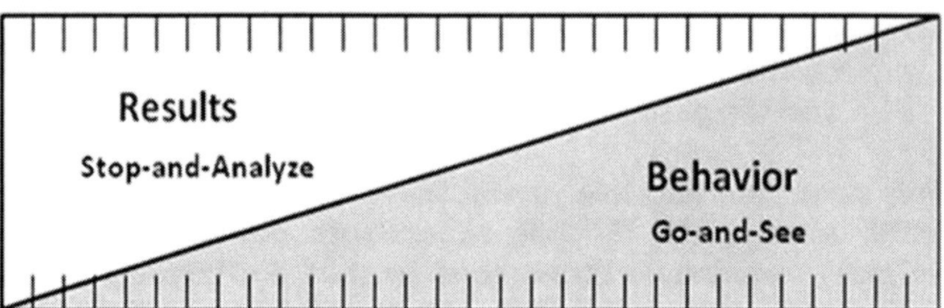

It is easy however to become over-reliant on hard indicators as they are easier to measure and can be monitored remotely. This becomes even more of a problem if on-job coaching is not an integral component of the management system.

Go and See

Approximately 60% of fast-moving consumer good's sales are made on impulse. Consumers make the purchase decision while in the store not before, based on factors like: availability, price, and presentation. These factors are soft indicators which need to be executed at the point of purchase--and to manage them you need to go-and-see.

Chart four summarizes the results of a survey conducted by the Economists Intelligence Unit with 102 international companies. These companies were asked if they were using or planned to use the six measures in the chart below.[1]

Chart 4

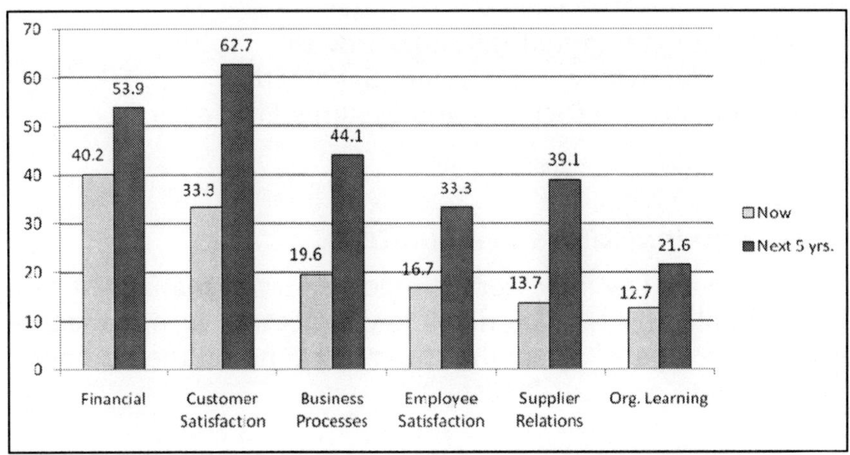

Notice that the measures most companies intended to start monitoring in the next 5 years were soft indicators. Financial measures were still important, but the most dramatic increases were with soft indicators. Respondents stated that more innovative indicators were needed to monitor work in progress, and to take timely corrective action.1

 *Key Indicators are Balanced*

Lopsided measures create lopsided performance. If we become too focused on one dimension of performance, we often pay for it elsewhere. For example, every production manager dreams of improving output. But if output measures aren't balanced with planned maintenance, output will eventually take a nosedive. Or if you push too hard to improve delivery efficiency (units delivered per hour) in a route delivery system, you will reach a point where accidents, errors, and customer satisfaction undermine efficiency gains.

It is easier to optimize performance when you have a balanced set of key indicators on your dashboard. This allows you to monitor the impact of one measure on the other and determine the best trade-off. Some indicators are in opposition, others complement each other. The following are examples of balanced measures:

- Cost Cutting and Revenue Growth
- Productivity and Customer Satisfaction
- Functional Efficiency and Systems Efficiency

Key Indicators are Limited

So, how many key indicators should you try to manage? There is no simple answer. Too many key indicators turn managers into "paper tigers," spending too much time on the numbers. This leads to a sluggish system.

On the other hand, if you don't use key indicators to manage performance, you can fall into the "activity trap" of responding to whatever comes across your desk, first-in-first-out, be it critical or trivial.

As chart 5 illustrates, a small number of key indicators, the critical few, account for a major proportion of the output or results.[2] The best companies have a few closely-watched-numbers.

Chart 5

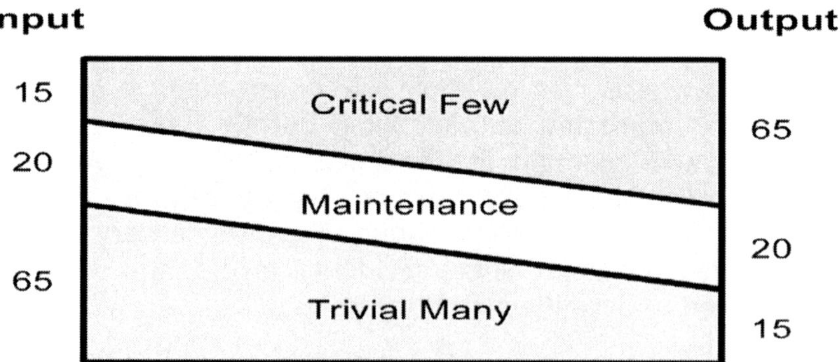

Many companies however monitor a lot of non-critical indicators. Some are maintenance indicators, some are trivial. Neither have a major impact on the bottom line. Even if they are managed perfectly, there is no great multiplier at work. While it may be politically incorrect to say so, sometimes you have to "let some fires burn". Just make sure they are non-critical.

Another factor to consider in determining how many key indicators you attempt to manage is the readiness of the team.

There is a big difference between measuring performance and managing performance.

If a team has had little experience managing its own performance, it is best to start with no more than three or four of the most critical key indicators. As confidence is gained in analyzing data, identifying the cause of variances, and generating solutions, more indicators can be added if needed.

Key Indicators are Controllable

Control, in this context, is the degree of authority a team has in managing its key indicators. When control is high, the team can: change a key indicator that is no longer relevant, take preemptive action to exploit an opportunity, or take corrective action to fix a problem.

The best companies place as much control as possible in the hands of those who are responsible for the key indicators. By now you will realize how important we believe this is - and how rarely we see it practiced.

Control is lost if it is centralized at the top, reducing both the quality and the speed of decision making. Control is also lost if it is given but not taken. This happens when those closest to the action lack the confidence or competence to use the authority they are given. Later in this chapter we will discuss a method for deliberately moving the control closer to the action.

Testing Key Indicators

The following questions can be used to test your key indicators against the five best practices.

1. Aligned Indicators

- Are you measuring the right things?
- Are key indicators aligned with the vision and strategy?
- Are key indicators aligned within and across functional lines?
- Is the responsibility for key indicators clear (who, what, when)?

2. Hard and Soft Indicators

- Are you over-managing hard indicators?
- Have you developed ways to measure soft indicators?

3. Balanced Indicators

- Are you achieving results in one area at the expense of another?
- Are you measuring internal productivity for each unit?
- Are you measuring customer satisfaction for each unit?

4. Limited Number

- Are you trying to manage too many key indicators?
- Are you focused on the critical few rather than the trivial many?
- Are you managing performance or just measuring it?

5. Controllable Indicators

- Are key indicators too centrally controlled?
- Do individuals and teams have enough control over their indicators?
- Do they have the competence to take control if it is given?

****

2. Three Types of Key Indicators

This section discusses functional, customer satisfaction, and execution key indicators.

Functional Key Indicators

These indicators measure functional productivity—input, process and output--and cascade down from each function's strategy and mission.

Customer Satisfaction Key Indicators

These indicators measure internal and final customer satisfaction. As illustrated in chart 6 every function should be held accountable for both functional productivity and customer satisfaction. Both should be measured in order to optimize performance. This is a far tougher proposition than just delivering functional results.

Chart 6

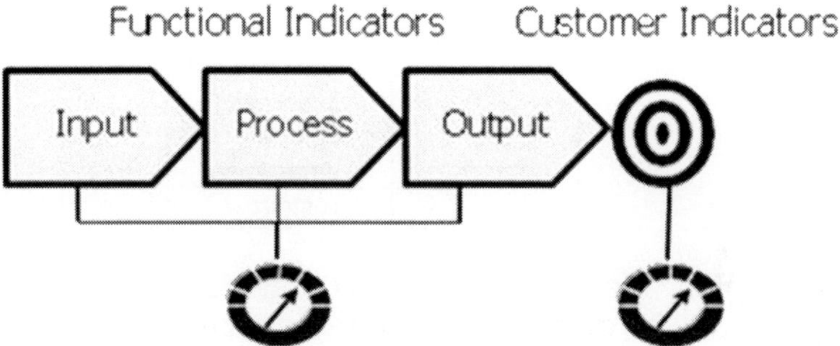

As we saw earlier, the Customer Maps & Mission intervention brings the supplier-customer discipline of the open market inside the organization. In developing its mission, each function meets with its customers to identify their *requirements.* This lays the groundwork for translating customer requirements into customer key indicators.

Some key indicators measure both functional productivity and customer satisfaction, most do not. Chart 7 illustrates what happens when functional teams sit down with their customers and explore ways to improve customer satisfaction. The three suppliers below discovered that their current measures were primarily focused on functional productivity (column 4) rather than on customer satisfaction.

Chart 7

1. Supplier	2. Customer	3. Product/ Service	4. Functional K.I.	5. Customer K.I.
Warehouse	Distribution, Delivery Drivers	Loading Trucks	• Loading Productivity • Timely--All trucks loaded by 6am	• Load Accuracy, per load sheet • Safe for transport • Conveniently placed for unload
IS	Marketing	Design software to track promotional effectiveness	On-time, on-budget delivery of new software	• Users Trained • Utilization of software
HR	All departments	Recruitment and Selection	• Monitor turnover • Post openings • Conduct initial interviews • Complete employment contract	• The time required to fill an opening

Each supplier identified customer satisfaction indicators in column 5, in discussions with their customers. In the warehouse example, distribution drivers were satisfied with the timely loading of trucks but not with the way they were being loaded.

In the Information Services (IS) example, software programs were being efficiently developed, but they weren't being used. After meeting with the marketing department, they learned that their designs were too complicated. They decided to make a bold move. As a supplier, they would start holding themselves accountable for the frequency of usage by the customer. They came up with a way of measuring how often users logged on to a program. In monitoring usage, they found the two biggest problems were poor design and un-trained users. Solving both became the responsibility of the IS function. Customer service came to mean much more than just slipping a new software program "under the door" as IS specialists ran off to the next project. The utilization of software programs by users turned out to be a key indicator with sharp teeth. It fundamentally redefined the IS mission and significantly improved the service to customers.

The HR department in this example did an excellent job of tracking its activities. It generated lots of reports that seemed to demonstrate that they were doing a terrific job of satisfying their customers. Their customers however indicated that they wanted empty positions filled quicker. This mattered more than the processes or paperwork as it related to recruiting and selection. The lost productivity because of unfilled openings far outweighed the additional effort required to fill them quicker.

In traditional organizations, internal customer satisfaction is rarely on the "performance dashboard." Yet breakdowns in delivering internal customer satisfaction are a major cause of poor strategy execution.

Disruptive boundaries crumble when every function is accountable for customer satisfaction as well as functional productivity.

Measuring Soft Indicators

A lot has been written about the limits of accrual accounting and the importance of work-in-progress measures. And there is a growing recognition that better indicators are needed to measure quality and service. Yet too often, soft qualitative indicators don't get much respect.

Few soft, qualitative indicators are monitored at the senior level. Some senior managers, while highly intelligent, have little operational experience. They prefer to manage performance by managing the hard numbers. IT groups as well don't always appreciate the need for both visual and electronic systems to monitor performance.

"...the best visual indicators are right at the work site, where they jump out at you and clearly indicate by sound, sight, and feel the standards and any deviation from the standards. A well developed visual control system increases productivity, reduces defects and mistakes...and generally gives the workers more control over their environment." [3]

From: The Toyota Way

In fact, some critical dimensions of performance can only be monitored by direct visual observation. Without a process to gather, quantify, and display visual indicators, they get lost. Then you fall into the trap of over-managing hard numbers. Pat Kerwin, a National Football League analyst, had this to say in evaluating a game:

"It didn't show up in the numbers, but it showed up on the video tape. You had to be on the sidelines to fully understand what really happened." [4]

Measuring soft indicators requires two things. First, expectations or standards need to be clearly defined in observable terms. This could include the key steps of a task, the start-up procedures for manufacturing equipment, or the standards for resolving a customer complaint. And second, a skilled observer/coach needs to "go and see" the actual performance compared to the expectation or standard. When it comes to soft measures:

You need to inspect what you expect.

The performer needs to understand the expectations and know how to achieve them; and the observer/coach needs a simple checklist that defines the expectations or standards, and also needs to be able to recognize them behaviorally in real-time. This will be discussed more fully in chapter 9 which deals with on-job coaching.

Three types of soft key indicators are illustrated in chart 8 below:

1. *Observe the Performance*--observing the performer as he or she is performing.

2. *Inspect Product or Service*
   - Inspecting products before they are delivered to the customer--internal quality checks conducted by the supplier to ensure products that leave the function meet or exceed customer requirements.
   - Inspecting services after they have been executed/ delivered--visually checking to ensure that current conditions are within standard. This involves observing the *outcome* of performance rather than observing the performance as it occurs.

3. *Survey*—using questionnaires to measure the level of satisfaction of those on the receiving end of the performance--the customer, the employee, the team.

Chart 8

Soft Indicators	
1. Observe Performance	• Meeting Leader Skills • Coaching Skills • Sales Presentation Skills • Resolving Customer Complaints
2A. Inspect Product Before Delivered	• Finished Product Quality • Financial analysis, reports
2B. Inspect Service After Delivered	• Good Manufacturing Practices(GMP) • Technical Repair • Merchandising
3. Survey	• Customer Satisfaction • Employee Satisfaction • Leadership Practices Feedback

Measuring soft indicators is not as difficult as it may seem, as long as there is agreement on what the desired behavior looks like. The appendix for chapter 10 contains a Review Standards Checklist, which is used to monitor the effectiveness of review meetings. It took several versions of the checklist before we got it right. And "right" does not mean perfect – it means good enough.

Execution Key Indicators

The dictionary definition of execution is: "to perform what is required, to carry out fully." There is little ambiguity in this straight-forward, action-oriented language. Yet some managers prefer the glamour-work of strategy to the heavy-lifting of execution; some are more concerned with managing-up than managing-down; and others just get caught-up in the "adminis-trivia" of attending meetings and writing reports.

Whatever the reason, not enough time is spent out on the job where things get produced and delivered to customers.

Recent research conducted in more than 1,000 companies in over 50 countries found that: *"Three out of every five companies rated their organization weak at execution."* [5]

So what is the manager's role in executing strategy? Our answer is quite simple: manage the system at your level and monitor the system at the level below you. It is the system that drives execution.

There is nothing new here. This is back to basics--whether you call it the chain of command or the linking-pin function. Most managers, however, are rewarded for "making their numbers," not for managing the system that delivers the numbers. The COBRA mantra is:

Show me the numbers, but also show me the system.

When we say show me the system, we mean quite literally that managers at every level should be prepared to demonstrate their management system at any time: to describe their strategic objectives and how they measure and monitor them; to demonstrate their coaching program out on the job; and to invite their supervisor to sit in their performance review meetings and evaluate their effectiveness. This is the type of rigor that is needed to build a simple, disciplined system. The system in the hands of competent leaders is the great flywheel of execution.

In developing COBRA, we have experimented with various ways to measure strategy execution. Chapter 9 will discuss on-job coaching. We recommend that managers at every level develop monthly coaching plans to deal with both the developmental needs of the team and current performance problems. The following key indicators can be used to monitor coaching:

- Coaching Plan—the percent completion of the monthly coaching plan, which involves both coaching your team and monitoring the coaching that is done by your subordinates.
- Coaching against a Variance—this is aimed at correcting a current performance problem, and is measured by the performance improvement after coaching occurs.
- Walking the Job—inspecting job standards with a check list.

Chapter 10 will discuss standards for conducting performance review meetings. Every unit manager is expected to conduct regular review meeting with his or her team, and to periodically sit-in on review meetings conducted by subordinates. Observing a review meeting, you can quickly determine if the manager is effective in solving problems, taking action, and rewarding results. The following key indicators can be used to monitor review meetings:

- Percent completion of plan to sit-in review meetings(verified by a recap report discussed in chapter 10)
- Review meeting effectiveness based on Review Standards Checklist

The best way to measure execution is an open issue. The above key indicators have proven effective, but there may be better and easier ways to do this. What counts is a commitment to improve execution and good old fashion trial and error learning.

3. Key Indicator Worksheet

In the previous section, three types of key indicators were discussed: functional, customer satisfaction, and execution. Chart 9 is a worksheet used to identify key indicators and how they will be measured and reviewed. In this example, the Team Leader (TL) is a first-line sales manager with a team of five sales reps. The Team Leader reports to an Area Manager (AM). In identifying key indicators, the team leader analyzed two documents: the sales department strategy and its unit mission, and then asked three questions:

- How do I measure functional productivity?
- How do I measure customer satisfaction?
- How do I measure market execution?

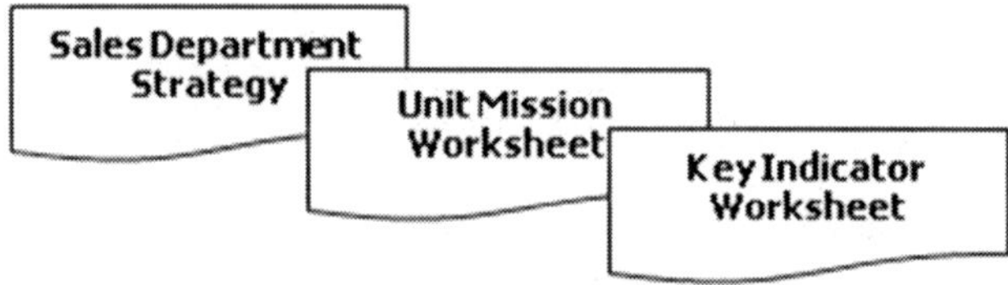

Chart 9

Key Indicator Worksheet				
Function: Sales	*Level: Team Leader*			
1. Type	*2. Key Indicators*	*3. Standards*	*4. How Measure?*	*5. Review*
F	• Sales volume by Area	TBD by month	SAP software	TL monitors daily, team review with reps weekly
F	Volume-Generating-Activities • Displays: number, quality	125 per week 25 per rep	• Self-report • Display Boards • Store Checks by TL	TL monitor daily, team review with reps weekly
C	• Merchandising Standards	90%	Store Checks by TL using Merchandising Stds.	Team review with reps weekly
C	• Retail Customer Satisfaction Survey	85% +	Survey/Interview quarterly ,150 retail outlets	Quarterly Team Review

E	**Coaching:** • TL conducts 6, ½ day on-route coaching sessions weekly(1 per rep)	% completion 90%	Plan Vs Actual Spot check by Area Mgr.	Area Mgr reviews TL coaching in monthly TL meeting
	Review: • TL Conducts weekly reviews with reps	Review Effectiveness Standards	Area Mgr. observes review meeting using Standards	Area Mgr reviews TL effectiveness in monthly TL meeting

Legend

1. Type: F=Functional, C=Customer, E=Execution

2. Key Indicators

- Functional Key Indicators--Volume targets are set monthly for the team and each sales representative. Volume-generating-activities change weekly.

- Customer Satisfaction--Customer satisfaction measures include regular assessments of the merchandising done by sales representatives in their retail outlets. Quarterly surveys are used to measure the satisfaction of retail customers.

- Execution Key Indicators--The Team Leader is in the market three full days a week (6, ½ day sessions) coaching sales reps, making store checks, and meeting with retail customers.

3. Standards/Targets

Setting standards and targets is influenced by:

- Historical performance/readiness
- Theoretical limits
- Industry benchmarking
- Market opportunities
- Competitive realities, etc

If you are repeatedly struggling to achieve the standards you have set, consider process improvement. As much as possible setting standards should be a collaborative process, a mix of top-down and bottom-up target setting.

4. How measure?

As you have seen this includes hard measures that are fed into a computer and soft measures like surveys and checklists.

5. Review

Review meetings are used to recognize positive results and to correct performance that is below standard. A rep that has sold only 15 displays is below target for the week and needs help getting back on target. Functional and customer satisfaction measures are reviewed by the Team Leader. Execution measures are reviewed by the Area Manager, the level above.

****

4. Risk/Readiness Matrix

This is a proven process for moving decision making as close as possible to the point of control. Those on the ground usually understand the situation better: the concrete details, the personalities, the constraints. They can quickly respond to fast-breaking problems and opportunities.

Decision-making can be divided into three basic areas: strategic decisions, day-to-day operational decisions, and human resource management decisions. The matrix is explained below:

Seek Input of Subordinates

A good time to have this discussion is after you and your subordinates have agreed on key indicators. Ask each subordinate if he or she needs more control, more decision making authority, to effectively manage their key indicators: to modify plans, change processes, redistribute resources. Listen to their suggestions and agree to get back to them after you have had time to consider their suggestions.

Rank Decisions by Risk

Make a list of the decisions you *might* delegate to your subordinates based on their input and yours. Rank these decisions in terms of the risk involved. Some decisions are routine and have low to moderate risk, like changing a work schedule. Others, like renegotiating a customer contract, involve more risk. The ranking will help you determine those decisions you may want to retain, those you may want to share, and those you may want to delegate.

Rank Decisions by Readiness

Next, rank each subordinate's readiness to make these decisions. Consider past experience and demonstrated skill in making decisions. In some cases, the subordinates will be low in readiness and need a lot of coaching. In other cases, they may have the confidence and experience to make sound decisions on their own.

Plot Decisions on Matrix

Plot the decisions on the matrix shown in Chart 10. Decisions in Quadrant 4, for example, are low in risk and the subordinate's readiness is high. So these decisions can be delegated now.

Chart 10

Risk/Readiness Matrix

High	**1. Don't Delegate** *Renegotiate chain agreements*	**3. Coach, Shared Decisions** *Changes to strategic plan for local market*
Risk	**2. Coach, Delegate soon** *Key customer presentation*	**4. Delegate Now** *Monitoring credit collection*
Low	***Readiness***	*High*

Delegate Appropriate Decisions

Share the matrix with the subordinate. If you are unsure of his or her readiness, ask a few questions to help you decide:

- Have you had experience making this type of decision?
- How would you go about making this type of decision?
- Would you feel confident making this type of decision?

Based on this discussion, delegate decisions in Quadrant 4 and discuss how you plan to deal with other decisions.

In summary, decision making autonomy between levels can range from:

- Supervisor makes decision, has little latitude, provides little explanation (Q1)
- Supervisor makes decision, but explains how decision was made. (Q2)
- Shared decision making with subordinate(Q3)
- Partial delegation: If this occurs, then do that.(Q4)
- Complete delegation: You make the call, but keep me in the loop.(Q4)

When you have completed this process, you will see real change - perhaps even dramatic change. The speed and quality of taking decisive action greatly improves when people on the ground have the competence and authority to make decisions. They are more engaged, more focused, and more enthusiastic.

Chapter Summary

We have yet to find a secret formula or a fail-safe equation for identifying key indicators. At its best identifying key indicators is a journey employing rational analysis and experimentation--a continuous search to find the simplest and most cost-effective way to measure performance. The advice of the wise tailor is fitting:

Measure Twice Cut Once

In summary, the five best practices are methods our most successful clients use in identify key indicators. The three types of key indicators - functional productivity, customer satisfaction, and strategy execution - keep the focus on the major drivers of sustainable performance. The key indicator worksheet provides a structured format for identifying key indicators. And, finally, the risk/readiness matrix helps move control closer to the action.

These concepts and tools will enable you to align key indicators with the strategy. This expedites the execution of strategy. Chapter 8 deals with performance tracking of key indicators.

Chapter 8
Performance Tracking

The system is an engine that runs on information.

Effective performance tracking serves to gather, process, and transmit information to the user in a timely, accurate, and understandable format.

Information can be used to develop strategy, monitor performance, and make sound decisions. This chapter will discuss:

1. Four Best Practices
2. The Tracking Audit
3. The Tracking Audit Worksheet

****

1. Four Best Practices

Exploit Information Technology

The world's best-run companies relentlessly pursue information technology, which helps to make them market leaders.

Without major advances in the exchange of information, a walls-down, global economy could never have emerged. Thomas Friedman describes these advances as the democratization of technology which is the result of: "...several innovations that came together in the 1980's involving computerization, telecommunication, miniaturization, compression technology and digitization."[1] This has had a major impact on how we gather, analyze and exchange information in our personal and business lives. Thanks to a host of increasingly portable devices, plus the infrastructure of the web, communication power and information access are available nearly everywhere, at any time, with practically anyone.

 *One, Integrated System*

An integrated tracking system that crosses regional and national boundaries provides a major competitive advantage. It enables the operational level of the organization to monitor performance and solve problems on a real-time basis. It also allows the executive level to plan and execute complex projects and programs that require the precise coordination of many different functions.

United Parcel Service (UPS), for example, ships 14.1 million packages all over the globe each day, using an integrated end-to-end tracking system. The system tracks each parcel through ten steps of the journey. Each station gets a daily report on the status of every package moving through it, along with a station-specific performance rating.

UPS Tracking System

1. The customer prints a UPS shipping sticker in their mail room. It automatically sends UPS all the shipping information.
2. UPS driver picks-up the package and scans the bar code on the sticker.
3. Package delivered and scanned at UPS center.
4. Packages travels on a conveyor belt which routes it to an outgoing truck where it is scanned.
5. Package is scanned as it is loaded into a bulk container called an igloo.
6. Igloo is scanned as it is loaded into a UPS plane.
7. Igloo arrives at UPS hub airport. It is unloaded, scanned and feed into another sorting system.
8. Package is scanned as it is loaded into igloo and igloo is scanned as it is loaded into UPS plane headed to final destination airport.
9. Igloo is scanned at final destination airport, unloaded and package is scanned. Then it is sorted by a conveyor, and scanned before it is transported to the city center by a tractor-trailer. Package is sorted and scanned before it is loaded into a UPS package car.
10. Driver delivers package to destination and scans to confirm delivery. The customer signs for package on the driver's hand-held computer.[2]

This is clearly an integrated tracking system that provides timely feedback on quality, productivity and customer satisfaction for every station throughout the company.

Information technology has had a tremendous impact on how companies manage their business, but it also has had its share of growing pains.

Fragmented tracking systems occur for a number of reasons. An IT user may tinker with a stand-alone PC application, if the main system is not providing the needed information. Or one function may install an off the shelf program that is not integrated with the main system. In other cases, the tracking system only provides information designed for the executive level, not the operational level. And sometimes mergers and acquisitions bring together systems that don't talk to each other. Over time, a patchwork develops. Pockets of valuable information exist in limbo, and they can't be mined.

In contrast to such randomness, companies with integrated tracking system generally have clear policies and standards for system development and management. And it pays off for them.

 *IT Providers and Users Collaborate*

Another best practice of well run companies is that IT providers and users work collaboratively to build an effective tracking system. Without such collaboration, breakdowns are likely, for which either side might be at fault. In some cases, IT users don't know enough about their information needs. In other cases, IT providers are bogged down in the nuts and bolts of technology and lack a commercial focus. According to a recent study by A.T. Kearney:

"The best IT ideas are not coming from IT, but from the business side." [3]

As discussed in chapter 4, the Customer Maps & Mission intervention is the best place to start in solving conflicts between internal suppliers and customers. Chart 1 illustrates a Customer Map for an IT function. Through the mapping process, this IT group gained a clear understanding of its role in supporting its customers.

Chart 1

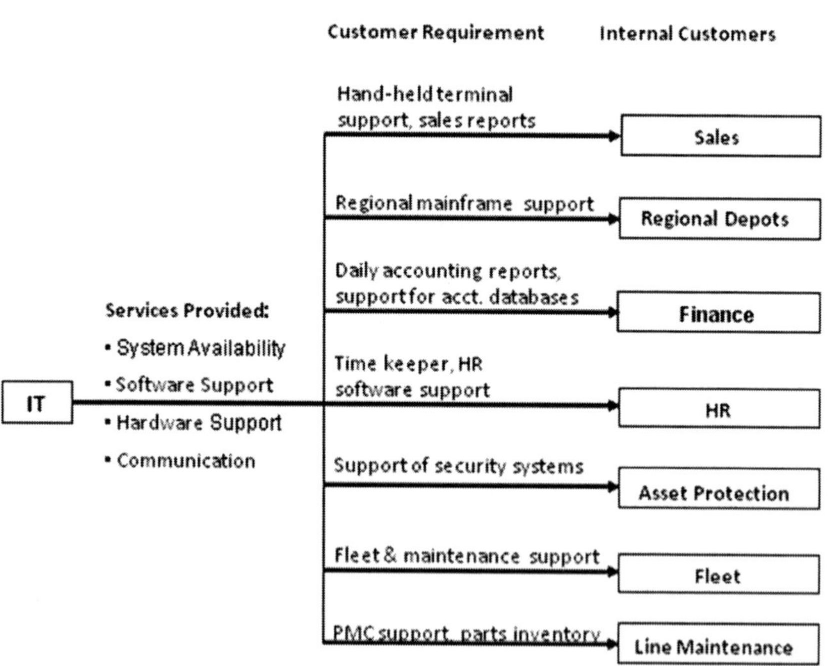

Even when the relationship between the user and the provider is good, conflicts still arise. One of the basic ground rules of the COBRA process is that each team manager has ultimate responsibility for developing a system to manage the team's performance. The manager owns it. If it doesn't work; the manager needs to fix it. And if managers can't get the necessary cooperation and support from other functions-- they need to jointly take the problem to the next level (to wave the red flag). It is not ok to say for example, "I can't get the information I need to manage the performance of my team."

The tracking system audit discussed later in this chapter will help information users assess their current tracking system and solve any problems.

Tracking is- Simple and Concise.

Effective performance management systems have balanced measures and balanced follow-up. This applies both to on-job coaching and the rigorous review of the numbers. Balanced follow-up eliminates the need for complex, elaborate tracking systems. A simple graph often will do. Information overload usually occurs in companies with a three rather than a five component performance management system—heavy on strategic plans, key indicators, and tracking reports--light on execution-focused coaching and review.

The Rule of Seven

Research shows that the human brain can handle only about seven pieces of information at a time. The quality of decision-making declines significantly with more information. Smart problem solvers walk away from the numbers when they are no longer useful. These managers know when to shift from rational/analytical problem solving to creative or experimental problems solving.

These four tracking best practices are consistently used by our most successful clients. They also rely on a COBRA tool called the Tracking Audit.

****

2. The Tracking Audit

The audit builds on the key indicator worksheet we covered in chapter 7. It helps managers identify the information they need to track their key indicators.

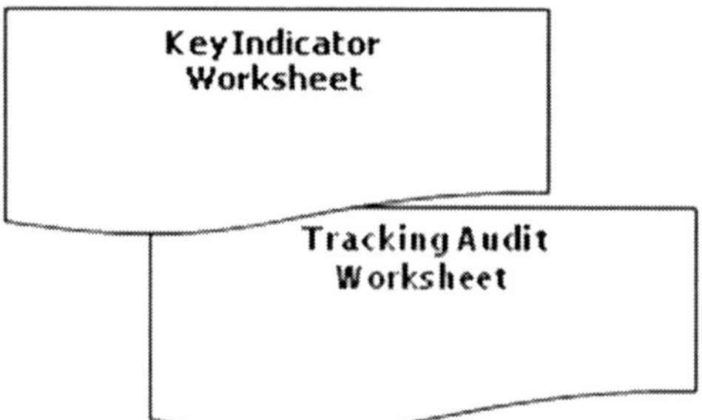

Three people need to participate in the audit: the IT user, the IT provider, and the general manager. The IT user determines the information necessary to track their key indicators. The IT provider's role is to understand the commercial needs of the user, the state-of the-art technology, and help provide *the best available tracking system*. The general manager is there to "break ties" and ensure that an integrated information system is being built. The audit answers six questions, which we will discuss below.

- Who needs the information?
- What information is needed?
- When is the information needed?
- Is the information displayed effectively?
- Is the information being accurately analyzed?
- Are the current hardware and software effective?

****

Who needs the information?

Here you determine who needs to monitor your unit's performance, beyond your team. For example, a sales team leader will share sales performance tracking with their area and general sales manager; internal suppliers will share customer satisfaction tracking with their customers.

What information is needed?

A key indicator may be expressed in absolute terms, or as a percentage, a ratio, or an index. All of this needs to be clarified. In addition, if a mathematical formula is used, care must be taken to ensure the formula is valid. We once made a study of ten manufacturing plants in the same industry, and encountered ten different ways to calculate line efficiency. All of the plants claimed to have 99-100% efficiency. Hello.

In the audit process, the question of *what* information is needed, is discussed separately from the question of *when* information is needed. In practice, however, the two questions are often determined concurrently. If the tracking system isn't delivering the right information at the right time, accountability is lost.

Rocket Man

The field sales team was having major problems getting new product listing actually stocked on the retailer's shelf. The national key accounts group negotiated new product listings directly at the head office of the super market chains. It was the field sales team's responsibility to ensure that new product listings were actually on the shelf throughout the country. In working with this client, we made many market visits and sat-in many monthly review meetings with area sales managers and their teams trying to solve the problem. The tracking system measured sales of existing products and sales of new products on a monthly basis for each sales area. But they had no way of measuring the <u>percentage of new product listings that were actually on the shelf, by sales rep, on a daily or weekly basis</u>. When negative variances were discussed bases on monthly, aggregate data for the area, the sales reps always had a way of avoiding responsibility:

- *My accounts are fine. It's the other reps that aren't performing.*
- *I just got an agreement from three of my accounts to reset the shelves so we can find space for the new listing. It won't appear on the report until next month.*
- *A lot of my accounts say they aren't getting the new listing reports from their head office.*

Some of these things may have been true, but performance remained below standard month after month. Though Area sales managers became more and more demanding, performance did not improve. The reps had figured out that the tracking system was incapable of holding them individual accountable.

After several all-night sessions with the general sales manager and an IT wizard called Rocket Man we cobbled together a program that could track the percentage of new product listings that were actually on the shelf by sales rep by day. It wasn't pretty but it got the job done. Area managers could now set new listing targets by week by rep and get feedback on a daily basis. The sales team went through all the classic stages of grieving--from denial, to anger, to grudging acceptance. They had nowhere to hide, the bulls eye now hung around each of their necks. Performance improved dramatically.

When do you need the information?

In determining when information is needed, there are several things to consider. Yes, you would like the information on demand whenever you want it. With some key indicators this is possible, but with others it may not be possible, or the cost may be prohibitive.

The primary consideration, however, is to determine how often you need to review a key indicator to optimize results. Each manager or supervisor needs to make this decision for their unit.

As a general rule you want information on key indicators soon enough to catch a problem early or to exploit an emerging opportunity. This, of course, all depends on the key indicator. You may want information on employee turnover and overtime on a monthly basis, and sales information on a daily or weekly basis. If you track and review information too often, you can over-correct normal variations.

So what is a normal variation? Developing control charts that establish average output and upper and lower control limits will help you answer the question. Control limits enable you to distinguish between normal variations and unacceptable variances. As W. Edwards Deming writes, "control charts stop people from chasing down causes" or over responding to normal variations.[4] On the other hand if you don't monitor key indicators frequently enough, small problems can become large problems. Your goal is to build an early-warning system.

Chart 2 is an example of a partial audit that deals with one sales key indicator. Notice that the team leader on the ground needs sales by week, by product, by package, and by sales rep, compared to target. With this information each team leader is prepared to conduct an effective weekly team review meeting.

Chart 2

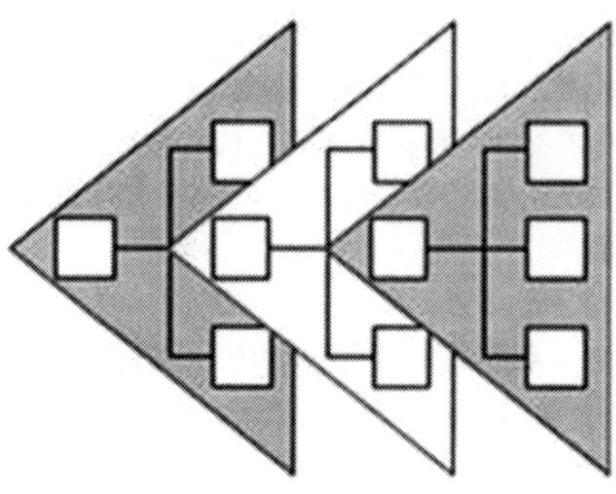

Who	What	When
General Sales Mgr. & Area Mgrs.	Total sales for the period by product and package for the total market and by area.	Monthly
Area Mgrs. & Team Leaders	Total sales for the period by product and package by area and by team	Biweekly
Team Leaders & Sales reps.	Total team sales for the period by product, by package, and by sale rep...compared to target.	Weekly

Slicing and Dicing

The ability of an information system to disaggregate information in real-time is critical. It enables sales managers, for example, to uncover the cause of a sales variance within minutes by unbundling the data in various ways: by sales area, by channel, by customer, by sales representative, by product, by package and so on. These variables must be designed into the software of course.

You may not always come out with a final answer when disaggregating data, but it gives you a big head start in your problem solving. When we conduct tracking audits with clients, we ask IT personnel if the current tracking system can disaggregate or unbundle variances in real- time. Their eyes usually light up and they indicate that yes, they have that capability.

Declan the Dis-agg-re-gat-or

Over a beer that night Declan assured us that their system could disaggregate sales reports in real time. It had all been programmed in, as he said, and you had only to ask the system for the information you wanted. We were pleased to hear this, and agreed to drop by for a demo the next day.

The next morning we pulled up the last monthly sales report and selected a sales area that was below target. We asked Declan to do what he could to unbundle the data and identify the key variances. He smiled broadly and disappeared. Several hours later he reappeared and indicated that he was having a few hiccups. He had pulled up a market segment report for the area which was useful in identifying under-performing segments, but this of course triggered more questions about sales by rep and by key customer in those segments. He smiled but less broadly and asked us to come by after lunch, and again disappeared.

By three that day reams of printouts cascaded from his desk. This he scowled is a sales report by sales rep by market segment. He indicated that they had recently reorganized the sales rep territories so the report would not be too accurate. He had also come up with a sales report by customer for the period but it was rank-ordered by volume not by segment or rep, so he would have to go in and manually identify outlets by segment. He said he would get someone on it tomorrow and that he would have everything together by the end of the week.

Is the information displayed effectively?

Tracking systems should communicate efficiently and with impact, not consuming a manager's time needlessly. Performance tracking usually involves plotting actual performance over time. This is communicated most clearly with a line chart and a data table. Line charts display current performance versus target and trends. Historical data and trends are useful in analyzing the cause of a variance. For example, chart 3 tracks customer product complaints per million units of output. Notice that in 2003 the organization was averaging slightly more than 4 complaints per month.

Chart 3

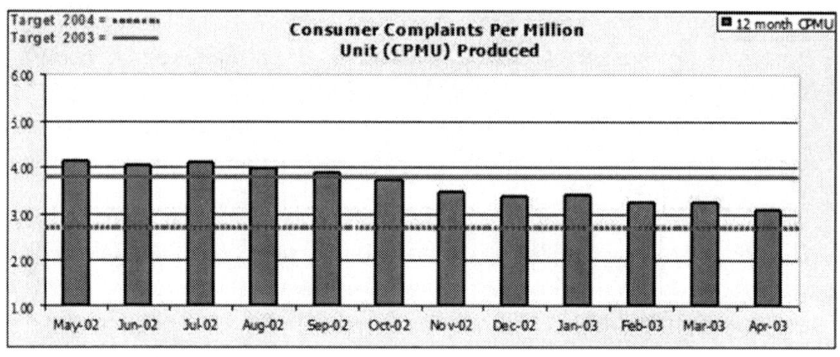

For the next year this client reset the target to achieve an even lower complaint rate. Though not yet on target, the company has improved over 2003 and is trending in the right direction.

As the management of the business is moved closer to the action, it is particularly important to have simple visual ways to track performance. We advocate the four foot rule. If the performers can't read a tracking display from four feet away, make it larger and simpler, whether on a computer screen or a bulletin board.

Tice's the Tracker

Tice is a soft drink industry legend in Holland. He is the supervisor of the pre-mix sanitation unit. Not what you would call the sexy end of the business. Tice and his team clean and sanitize returnable five gallon beverage containers. They have the highest productivity in Northern Europe. I was pleased to receive an invitation to observe his operation. I envisioned a highly automated line with in-line logic processors and a control panel like a 747. What I saw was essentially a manual operation. Returnable stainless steel containers stacked on wooden pallets moved along a conveyer belt. They were loaded into the washer by hand and checked and tested after the washer. Then they were loaded back onto pallets and moved on to the filling station. As I scanned the room I didn't see any control panels, computers, or printouts. I did notice a brown paper bag tacked to the wall. Every so often Tice would walk over to the bag and make a mark. The crew seemed very focused and efficient. Periodically they would glance in the direction of the bag which hung next to the wall clock. At 11:45A the washer stopped and the team let out a cheer.

When I joined the team for lunch, I learned that Tice set improvement targets each month, and tracked output with a grease pencil on a brown paper bag. The lunch period started once the morning target had been achieved. That day they were fifteen minutes early for lunch.

Is the information being accurately analyzed?

A tracking audit also includes the human factor, specifically the competence and integrity of the user. Even when the data display is as simple as possible, data analysis skills are still needed to solve problems.

You need to read with your light on.

In manufacturing, line utilization is expressed as a percentage of perfect utilization, which is 100%. Low utilization can be caused by various factors such as poor scheduling and poor preventive maintenance. Chart 4 demonstrates an actual case.

Question: *What is the biggest cause of low Line Utilization?*

Chart 4

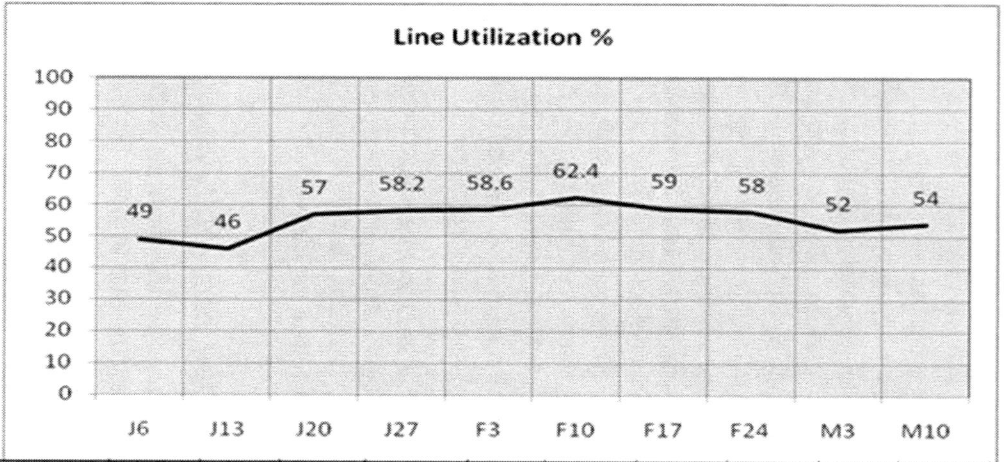

Line Utilization %

		J6	J13	J20	J27	F3	F10	F17	F24	M3	M10
Line Utilization		49	46	57	58.2	58.6	62.4	59	58	52	54
Available Time/hrs.		40	40	40	40	40	40	40	40	40	40
Lost Time %:	Breaks	6.3	6.6	6.6	6.8	6.8	6.4	6.8	6.9	6.4	6.6
	Start-up	6.4	6.6	7.1	7.4	6.6	6.2	6.9	6.7	6.3	6.4
	Clean-up	6.6	6.1	5	4.4	3.2	4.4	6.6	6.8	6.9	6.3
	Change over	11.3	17	4.4	2	6	5.9	1	3.7	12	12.3
	Mechanical	20.4	17.7	19.3	21.2	18.8	14.7	19.7	17.9	16.4	14.4

Those who take the longest time to solve the case are usually very methodical. They start at the top row of the data table and scan across and then down. Those who solve the case the quickest do the following:

1. First they look at the graph and identify the best week (F10) and the worst week (J13).
2. Then they scan down just those columns looking for the greatest differences for each lost time category.
3. They quickly notice that 17% of the lost time in J13 was due to change overs and only 5.9% in week F10.
4. Finally they scan across the change over row comparing change over downtime with weekly efficiency to confirm their findings.

The identification of the cause of low utilization only takes a few seconds. Such cases are useful in assessing the data analysis skills of IT users. This step of the audit also tests the competence of managers in using the current software programs to solve problems and make objective, un-biased decisions.

Integrity

Integrity is the glue that holds personal and business relationships together. It is a core value in most organizations, and should be in all. Integrity involves communicating in an authentic, straight-forward manner with customers, employees and the public at large. When integrity is compromised, trust disappears. This is another instance in which the culture and the system must be in alignment.

"If you torture the numbers long enough, you can get them to confess to anything." [5]

Integrity in tracking is serious stuff. If the numbers are distorted or manipulated to rationalize poor performance, the organization is in trouble, as Enron and WorldCom have shown. Companies that truly value integrity have no tolerance for those who distort data. Consequences are usually swift and serious. Quoting Deming again, the acid test is, "can you look into the mirror and say I want to know the truth." [6]

Does the current hardware and software meet your needs?

Hardware and software can take many different forms. Soft indicators may be tracked with manual, visual systems. Though these may be slightly less precise than a computer program, they are good enough. Stand-alone PCs may be used to track indicators that can't be tracked any other way. And, of course, there is the main company system, whether networked PCs or a main frame.

Any of these systems can give you timely, accurate information to manage performance. But, any of these systems can also fall short. Corporately, you need one integrated system that moves information quickly and accurately across the organization and around the world. Aggressive marketing programs, for example, require simultaneous information on inventory levels, sales forecasts, production plans, and competitive activity.

Each team needs the *best available system* to run its business. No team wants to hear about star-wars-solutions that are years away. The best available system may be a stand-alone PC application for the next six months until a new software program can be written. All of these options should be considered in developing the best tracking system for your team.

****

3. Tracking Audit Worksheet

In this final section of the chapter, we focus on the tracking audit worksheet used to record the findings of the audit. The worksheet illustrated in chart 5 provides a format for answering the six audit questions.

Chart 5

Tracking Audit Worksheet											
1. Who	2. What	3. When	4. Current System					5. Accurate	6. Format	7. Timely	8. Improvements/ Best-Available-System
			A	B	C	D	E				
A, B, C	Distribution: Truck Day Average by route and area	D, W		X				S	US	S	Need a simple PC system that can bundle and unbundle historical data for analysis
A, B, C	Distribution: Full Goods Returned by route and area	D, W			X			S	US	US	Data from Route Settlement is entered on PC Stand Alone. Need program to do this electronically.
A, B, C, D	Distribution: Trucks clean and empties sorted by route/area	D, W			X			S	HS	HS	Visual inspection by Warehouse Checker with a manual checklist is adequate.
A, B, C, D	Distribution: Route Settlement Errors by Driver	D, W					X	HS	S	HS	Dart 2 system is adequate.

A, B, D	Marketing: Setting promotional price	M	X					---	---	---	Develop Category Mgmt. software and obtain scan data from major supermarket chains to develop price elasticity models
A, B	Sales: Unbundling sales data	W, M			X			US	US	US	Develop software program that can disaggregate sales by area, rep, customer, product, etc. in real-time

This worksheet is a compilation of three audits by the distribution, marketing and sales functions. It includes three distribution key indicators, one marketing key indicator and one sales key indicator.

As you conduct an audit, it is helpful to build on information from your key indicator worksheet discussed in chapter 7.

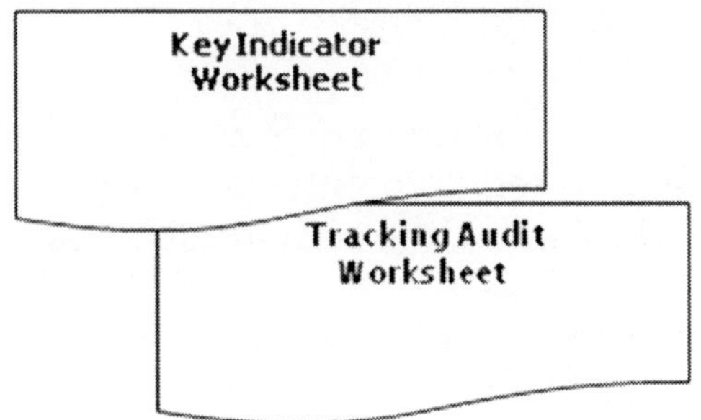

Legend

The following definitions are used to complete the worksheet:

1. Who needs to receive a tracking report for this key indicator?
   A= Your Supervisor, B= Team Leader/Team, C= Supplier, D= Customer

2. What key indicator and what information are needed?

3. When is the tracking report needed in order to manage performance? D=daily, W=weekly, M=monthly

4. Current System--What is the current tracking system: A=No System. B=Manual System (pencil & paper), C=PC Stand Alone, D=Networked PCs, E=Mini/Main frame

5. Accurate--Is the information accurate and in a form you can use (unbundled)? Select one of the following: Highly Satisfied (HS), Satisfied (S), or Unsatisfied (US).

6. Format--Is the display of information easy to understand? Simple graphics, clear standards, historical data tables? Select one of the following: Highly Satisfied (HS), Satisfied (S), or Unsatisfied (US).

7. Timely--Is the current system timely? Can you get it when you need it to manage performance? Select one of the following: Highly Satisfied (HS), Satisfied (S), or Unsatisfied (US).

8. Recommended Improvements--what is needed to meet your information requirements based on your response to questions 1-7? What is the best-available-system for now?

Once your team (the IT user) has completed columns 1-7, your information needs will be clear. At this point you should get your IT provider's help in solving any problems that have come up.

Chapter Summary

Effective performance tracking serves to gather, process, and transmit information to the user in a timely, accurate, and understandable format.

At the team level, performance tracking communicates actual results versus target, while at the company level it reveals how well the strategy is being executed. With this information you can detect trends, solve problems, and make sound decisions.

Next we will discuss on-job coaching, the fourth component of the performance management system.

Chapter 9
On-Job Coaching

A Sacred Cow That Goes Hungry

Review meetings (next chapter) are for analyzing and problem-solving. Coaching is about getting up, going out to observe, and helping your people get better at their jobs.

When COBRA was first developed, there were four components in the performance management system. On-job coaching was the missing piece, just as it is missing in far too many companies.

All of our clients had training departments and many had some sort of coaching or mentoring program. But these programs tended to be fairly unstructured and often had a short life cycle. Although we were slow learners, over time we came to understand the value of structured coaching and the need to integrate it into the system.

When an organization has a seasoned workforce and is operating in stable times, it can usually succeed with a moderate level of coaching. In turbulent times, however, when products, processes and technology are constantly changing, coaching is essential. The power of on-job coaching comes from the ability to transfer knowledge and skill consistently and immediately to the people who need it to execute.

A phone call from Nikos, who was responsible for implementing COBRA in Greece and other European countries, led us to add coaching to our management system.

Nikos Calling

"Listen, we've got the management system up and running in the Athens' operation but we still aren't making our numbers. There are a lot of new faces around here. Many of our most experienced managers and supervisors have been sent off to run newly acquired operations in other countries. The strategy and the key indicators are clearly defined. And the review meetings are very rigorous. There is nowhere to hide if you aren't performing. Yet we're not making our numbers and morale is very low."

After lengthy discussions with the management team in Greece, a decision was made to pilot an on-job coaching program. This turned the tide. It was the missing piece of the management system. With just four components, the system generated heat but not enough light. Both motivation and results increased dramatically once coaching was added to the system.

This chapter will discuss:

1. Four Best Practices
2. Coaching Styles
3. Developing an On-Job Coaching Capability

****

1. Four Best Practices

◎ *On-Job Coaching is a Key Component of the System.*

On-job coaching is a sacred cow that goes hungry. Everyone agrees that coaching is a great idea, but few do it well. Coaching programs often are launched as feel-good, stand-alone initiatives that quickly wind down. Companies that excel at coaching however, integrate it into the management system. It becomes part of the routine. Every manager is held accountable for coaching. It is a closely-watched performance indicator.

"A negative variance caused by a skill deficiency that surfaces in a weekly team meeting, automatically becomes part of the Team Leader's coaching plan for the next week. That's the way the system works."

Mr. Christos Tsolkas,
Director Regional Sales Strategy
Eastern Europe & Africa,
Philip Morris International

Coaching improves Strategy Execution

The best companies have figured out that on-job-coaching provides three important ways to improve the execution of strategy.

- *Improving Performance*

Unlike training programs, coaching solves performance problems in real time on the job. If the coaching is effective, performance improves - and it shows up in the numbers. If not, the coach is on the hot-seat

- *Monitoring Soft Indicators*

As discussed in chapter 7, some of the most important key indicators are soft: service quality, business processes, and market execution to name a few. Monitoring soft indicators requires that managers "inspect what they expect." This means creating observable standards and getting out on the job to monitor performance first hand.

- *Staying Close to the Customer*

Coaching has the additional benefit of putting the coach in regular contact with customers. For example, while a coach is on-site observing a sales call, he or she can also meet directly with retail customers and discuss any issues or concerns.

The same is true with non-sales functions and internal customers. A CFO observing one of her accountants present a budget report to an internal customer has the opportunity to discuss the level of customer satisfaction.

When on-job coaching is effective, employees come to realize that their manager will be around to *inspect what they expect.* They also realize that good performance will be praised, and they will get help with problems.

Time to Coach

There are no hard and fast rules on how much time is needed for coaching. It depends on a variety of factors: complexity of the task, readiness of the performer, competitive threats, and so on. Larry Bossidy and Ram Charan recommend that leaders at all levels spend as much as 40% of their time developing people.[1] Field sales managers in the best fast moving consumer goods companies spend an average of three days a week, or 60% of their time, out in the market coaching their team. Jack Welch, the former CEO of GE, has this to say about coaching [2]:

> ***"The team with the best players usually does win. And that is why, very simply, you need to invest the vast majority of your time and energy as a leader in three activities. You have to evaluate—making sure the right people are in the right job, supporting and advancing those who are, and moving out those who are not. You have to coach —guiding, critiquing and helping people to improve their performance in every way, and finally, you have to build self-confidence—pouring out encouragement, caring and recognition."***

In one operation that was having problems with market execution; we found that field sales managers were spending too much time at their PCs responding to e-mail requests for information from other functions. After some problem-solving with all parties concerned, the Commercial Sales Manager posted a new policy:

> ***"Unless it is a real emergency, field sales managers will not respond to any requests for information received on Tuesday through Thursday of each week. They will***

be in the market place on those days and should not be disturbed. Please copy me on any emergency requests."

This policy worked quite well. Field sales managers had the time to coach and had no excuses for not coaching. Companies with excellent on-job coaching programs usually have worked their way through these kinds of issues.

Training the Coach

Anytime a manager is out on the job discussing performance with an employee, it is a good thing. But some managers do a better job than others, and they're the ones who have received training on how to coach. They don't just rely on instinct.

The lion never makes a mistake, only the lion trainer.

Chart 1 illustrates our first-hand observations of effective and ineffective coaches.

Chart 1

Effective Coaches	*Ineffective Coaches*
Coach prepares for a coaching session by reviewing the job standards related to the performance problem, etc.	Coach not prepared.
Coach watches their people perform to determine their current readiness before intervening.	Coach jumps in and starts coaching or does the job for them.
Coach adapts their style to the situation: • Style 3 Participation-- ask, listen • Style 2 Persuasion—sell, teach • Style 1 Directing—tell, assert (see chart 3 below)	Coach gets stuck in one leadership style, often style 1.
Tell, Show, Do, Solo: Coach moves from telling, to demonstrating, to having the performer rehearse the task before doing it on their own for the first time.	Tell Only: Coach talks too much—does a "data dump"

These then are the four best practices we have observed in companies that do the best job of coaching their people. Coaching styles will be discussed next.

****

2. Coaching Styles

Developing people is a journey from dependence to independence. As illustrated in chart 2, a range of coaching styles is needed to move people "up the steps."

Chart 2

Moving Up the Steps

READINESS					
High				***Style 4***	*Delegate*
			Style 3	*Solo* *Involve*	
		Style 2	*Feedback* *Build Skills*		
Low	***Style 1***	*Set Goals* *Assess* *Readiness*			

With permission of Keilty, Goldsmith and Company

Styles

Readiness is the learner's ability and motivation for a specific task. Any coaching effort should start with an assessment of the learner's current readiness. The assessment can be done in several ways:

- Past experience—has the performer done the task before? How effectively?
- Direct observation—Coach observes performer on the job
- Interview—Coach asks questions to determine the other's motivation and ability to perform the task

Once the readiness is known, the coach can select the most appropriate style and move the learner up the development steps. If readiness is low, the coach will start with style 1 and 2—setting goals and building skills. If readiness is high, the coach will move quickly up the steps toward delegation (S3 & S4).

This leadership model was developed by Keilty, Goldsmith and Company. It is derived from the Leadership Contingency Model pioneered by Fred Fiedler[3] and popularized by Hersey and Blanchard[4].

The remainder of this chapter provides a process for implementing on-job coaching in your company.

****

3. Developing an On-Job Coaching Capability

This is a five step process:

- Gain Management Commitment
- Identify Coaching Needs
- Develop Coaching Plan
- Prepare to Coach
- Conduct Coaching

Gain Management Commitment

The executive team must first decide if they want to make coaching a strategic priority. Practically every strategic objective calls for on-job coaching: new technology, an acquisition, restructuring, productivity improvement, quality improvement, customer service, etc. A cost/benefit analysis will help confirm that a coaching program is a good investment. If the decision is made to move ahead, the next step is to specify the coaching needs of each unit.

Identify Coaching Needs

Analyzing needed competencies can become a hair splitting, academic exercise if taken too far. Tread carefully. Most coaching needs can be identified by line managers in two ways:

- *Coaching-Against-a-Variance*--involves coaching to correct a variance in performance caused by a skill deficiency. The variances generally surface in a performance review meeting. Warning! - the first response is often "send the employee to training." Resist this temptation, and get out there on the job with the person.
- *Developmental Coaching*--involves a planned, on-going program to build the core competencies of your people.

A key tool in developmental coaching is the skills audit. This is a simple, practical way to identify the coaching needs of your team.

Chart 3 is a skills audit for a shift leader on a production line. It was developed in one hour by a group of line managers. They first identified the most important skills of a shift leader. Then they selected a shift leader they had all worked with and assessed his readiness for each skill. The greatest coaching needs involved management skills (6 & 7 on the chart) rather than technical or people skills. A coaching plan was developed and implemented.

Chart 3

Skills Audit Position: Shift Leader Name: A. Jones	***Readiness***
1. Start-up and change over	High
2. Error diagnosis	High
3. Maintaining hygiene and safety standards	High
4. Maintaining product quality standards	Mod
5. Coaching and people development	Mod
6. Shift reporting	Low
7. Reviewing and solving performance problems	Low

No matter what the function or level, this straight-forward approach usually is sufficient for identifying developmental coaching needs.

Develop a Coaching Plan

Next, coaching needs should be translated into a coaching plan. Some teams make plans on a weekly basis, while others plan on a monthly basis and revise it weekly as required. The plan is developed by the team leader with input from the rest of the team to ensure agreement on dates, times and objectives.

At the end of the planned coaching period, a copy of the plan is sent to the coach's supervisor showing performance improvements and the percentage of the planned coaching that was actually conducted. This becomes a discussion item in the monthly review. Chart 4 is an example of a weekly on-job coaching plan for an Area Sales Manager.

Chart 4

Coach: *J. Cullen, Area Sales Manager* Percent Completion of Plan:				***On-Job Coaching Plan*** Week of: *06/06/2008*				
Sales Rep.	Date	Time	Location	Coaching Method			Standards Checklist	Comments
				Shadow	Car Coach	Store checks		
D. Fox	06/06	9-12 am	Tescos,#21	Plan Call			Planned Call Standards	
B. Murphy	07/06	1-4 pm	Area 3			Petro Stations	Merchandising Standards	
S. Turner	09/06	9-12 am	Safeway#37		Sell re-set		Sales Call Standards	

As you will note, on-job coaching for the field sales function typically involves three methods:

Shadowing: the coach observes the sales rep calling on retail customers and provides feedback based on the sales call standards.

Car Coaching: the coach helps the sales rep prepare, rehearse and conduct a sales call for a specific product or service - sell a promotion, a display, a reset, etc. The coaching usually occurs in the car outside the outlet.

Store Checks: the coach does store checks to observe merchandising standards and meet with customers. The coach may or may not be accompanied by the sales rep. Coaching occurs after the store-checks.

In companies that take coaching seriously, execution of the coaching plan is a key indicator - a closely watched number that has real consequences.

Ramon Checks Both Ends of the Board

Ramon wears an old Stetson hat, and raises a few head of cattle on the side. He is the Sales Manager of the Houston operation. He isn't much on paperwork or hanging out in the office. Not your corporate type, but awfully good. Ramon reviews results posted on the bulletin board each day as he heads out to the market. In March sales were flat, and Ramon pulled his sales supervisors in for a meeting.

"We need to get back to basics. Our plans and programs are fine; we just aren't executing them very well. The selling and merchandising need to improve. I want all of you to spend a lot more time out in the market coaching your people. You decide how you want to do it, just keep it simple. All I ask is that you develop a weekly plan indicating who's being coached on what. You can post it on the far end of the bulletin board."

Things went well for awhile. Supervisors were out their coaching and results improved. They posted their weekly coaching plans without exception, but some were better than others in executing the plans. The smart ones had figured out that coaching was something they needed to be doing, whether someone was asking for it or not. After a few months, however results started to slide again in some areas. One day Ramon asked Lefty, the supervisor for East Houston, to join him at the bulletin board. They had talked several times before. Lefty's results weren't good and Ramon had been out in his area enough to know that execution hadn't improved much.

"Lefty I'm a little confused, when we look at your results at this end of the board we see that your team is still doing poorly in selling the multi-pack promotion. But when we go down to the other end of the board, we see from your coaching plan that you have spent the last two weeks coaching them on selling the multi-pack promotion. Que pasa? I don't understand."

Lefty looked like he'd been kicked off the gallows on a short rope. Word got around pretty quick. If you're having performance problems, you'd better put it in your coaching plan. And if you put it in your coaching plan, you damn well better be doing the coaching, and results had damn well better improve...cause Ramon checks both ends of the board, amigo.

Prepare to Coach

At this point in building a coaching capability, you have gained the commitment of management, identified the coaching needs, and developed a coaching plan. Now it is time to prepare to coach.

The preparation will vary depending on the competence of the coach. Great coaches are more than great players. In sports, great players have mastered the task. They can perform it as well as anyone. Great coaches, however, have not only mastered the task, they have also mastered the content. They understand the standards and can break the task down into key behaviors, tips and techniques.

The following four steps help prepare the coach. The process rarely takes more than an hour. Once the planner worksheet is complete, it can be filed and used again and again.

- *Identify the Coaching Objective*

The coaching objective answers the question: What will the person be able to do at the end of the coaching session to demonstrate they have learned the new skill? The coaching objective helps the coach prepare and also provides a way of evaluating the effectiveness of the coaching.

- *Analyze Task or Content*

Once the coaching objective has been determined, the next step is to analyze the key steps of the task. If the coaching objective is to facilitate a meeting, the task analysis identifies the key steps in facilitating a meeting. The coach must be able to explain the steps of the task as well as demonstrate them. The learner must understand the task as well as perform it. Learning is more than imitation – "getting it" is the goal. The learner needs a mental map of the task, a way of framing and retaining the sequence of sub-tasks. When this is achieved, the learner is consciously competent. Chart 5 is an example of a coaching session planner for facilitating a meeting.

Chart 5

Coaching Session Planner	
1. Identify Coaching Objective: *Capable of facilitating a meeting after the coaching*	
2. Analyze Task: *b. Gather input for agenda from team* *c. Create and circulate agenda* *d. Start meeting on-time* *e. Review agenda & introduce topic leaders* *f. Ensure all members contribute* *g. Summarize and note any key decisions* *h. Draft and circulate meetings notes in two days*	***3. Design Coaching:*** *Tell: Describe each step and get feedback* *Show: Ask learner to sit in your meeting the next day and observe the key steps of task* *Do: Ask learner to prepare using the keys steps. Coach will sit in back of room and provide support and feedback after the meeting.*
	4. Evaluation: *Coach sits in learner's meetings for the next 3 weeks and provides feedback and support.*

• *Design Coaching Session*

Next you need to determine how you will conduct the coaching. When coaching involves building new skills, we have found the tell-show-do-solo method very effective. Retention studies have repeatedly demonstrated the effectiveness of this approach. Learners retain only 20% of what they hear--when the coach does most of the talking. But they retain 90% of what they hear, see, and do. Behavioral science research isn't the only validation of this principle.

When I hear, I forget;
When I see, I remember;
What I do, I understand

Confucius 451 B.C.

• *Evaluate*

The final step of preparing to coach is to determine how to evaluate the effectiveness of the session. There are various ways to do this. The coach and the learner can set a performance improvement target. The coach can routinely observe the performer on the job. Or if the coaching is based on correcting a key indicator variance, then reducing or eliminating the variance will be the measure of success. Now we are ready to coach.

• ***Conduct Coaching***

With your coaching session planner in hand, you are ready to go. The example that follows involves skill building using the tell-show-do-solo method. The objective is to prepare a sales rep to sell a new product to existing customers.

Here's the situation. The performance of the sales rep has been below target, so this is an example of coaching against a variance. Most of the coaching occurs in the sales representative's car outside the retail outlet. Once the coaching objective is set, two or three retails outlets that need the new product are identified. The coach and the sales rep drive to the first outlet. The task is to execute the five-step sales call (needs, benefits, overcoming potential objections, profit story, close). The *car coaching* method involves six steps

- Confirm Coaching Objective
- Tell
- Show
- Do
- Solo
- Feedback

****

√ Confirm Coaching Objective

The coach and the sale rep enter the first outlet and take a quick look around. They observe the current product offerings, the competition, and the type of consumers. This confirms that the coaching objective is appropriate for this outlet. Then they return to the car and the coach defines the objective: to prepare the rep to sell a new product to the customer. The coach sets it up this way:

"I am going to spend some time coaching you before you make the call on this outlet. The practice is exactly what you need. You have nothing to worry about. Once you are comfortable rehearsing the call with me, we will go inside. I'll be with you all the way."

√ Tell

The coach explains the five steps of the sales call. To ensure the message is being received, the coach asks for feedback. The coach avoids using closed questions that can be answered with a yes or a no answer (Do you understand?). Instead he uses open questions or "fill in the blank" questions to test for understanding (walk me through the key steps of the call). Once the coach is confident that the message has been received and understood, he moves on. At this point, the learner should understand the steps of the call and have a general idea of what they entail. If this is the case, they are on target.

√ Show

Next the coach shows the sales rep how to make the call. The rep gets to see each step enacted behaviorally. This is done using a role play in which the coach takes the role of the sale rep and the sales rep is the retail customer. The coach follows the five-step path and demonstrates each step in detail---use of the sales presenter, calculating the profit story, overcoming objections, etc. When the learner is comfortable with the sequence and content of the call, it's time to move on.

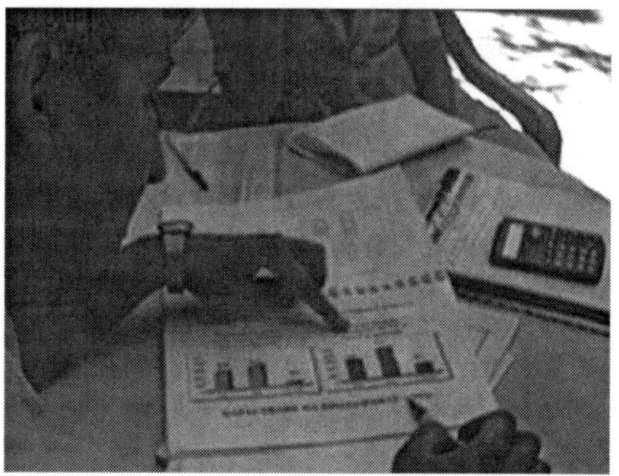

√ Do

Here the learner does the task for the first time as part of the coaching session. At this point the coach and the rep reverse roles. After several rehearsals the rep is usually ready to make the call, or go solo. The tell-show-do steps take place in the car. For the first call, the coaching usually takes about thirty minutes, after that it rarely takes more than ten minutes.

√ Solo

Soloing is the first time the learner performs a new task on the job. If the coaching has been effective, the learner usually has both the confidence and the competence to be successful. The coach is primarily there for support, and should not get involved unless the rep is really struggling. After the call when back in the car, the coach can provide feedback.

√ Feedback

When done properly, car coaching will result in a successful sales call. The smile on a rep's face coming out of the outlet is the ultimate metric. It is a smile of victory, of emerging confidence--and of relief. The rep's first words are usually, 'Let's go to the next outlet.' After the coach provides feedback on the call, they move on to make the same call with the two other customers.

Performance improvement for this newly acquired skill will be monitored at the next weekly review meeting.

Chapter Summary

In a competitive marketplace where products, services, and processes are constantly changing, coaching is indispensable - as well as the most productive use of a manager's time.

Everyone agrees that coaching is a good idea, but few do it well. It is a sacred cow that goes hungry.

In the best-run companies, on-job coaching is more than a good idea, it is a strategic imperative. It is part of every manager's job description, and is a closely watched performance indicator.

This chapter provides all the tools and techniques you need to develop an on-job coaching capability.

Chapter 10
Performance Review

A Checkpoint on the Execution Highway

The performance review is a regular, face-to-face meeting at the end of each performance period to monitor key indicators, analyze variances, and implement solutions. Whether it occurs in the field, on the production line, or in the board room, the review meeting is the nerve center of the management system.

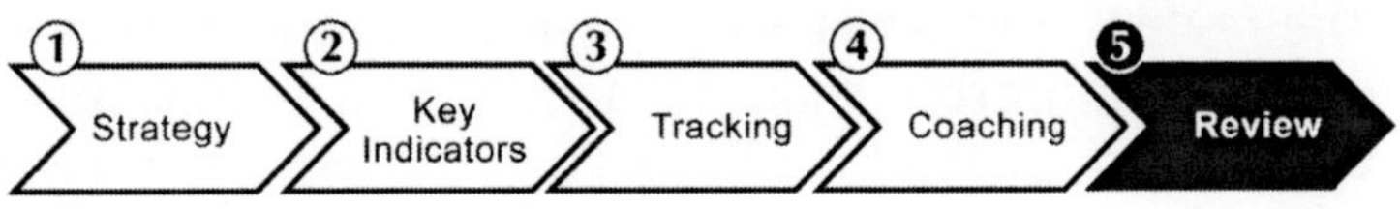

The agenda of the review is to evaluate wins, losses and opportunities of the current performance period and apply these learnings going forward.

Personal accountability and consistency are the hallmarks of effective performance review. The team leader asks the same questions every time:

- How are you doing versus target?
- If there is a variance, why?
- What are you going to do about it?
- Or better yet, what have you done about it?

In addition, the review meeting tests the integrity of the system. Is the strategy clear? Are the key indicators aligned with the strategy? Does the tracking system deliver accurate and timely information on current performance? There is no quicker way to determine if those that report to you have an effective management system than to sit-in their review--more on that later.

For reviews to be effective, the manager in charge must be a competent leader and problem solver. He or she must work to make the review a regular, expected discipline, respected by everyone who participates.

Once the review standards are embedded in the culture, team members know better than to arrive at a review meeting with unresolved problems. They continuously monitor their key indicators, analyze the reason for variances and make necessary corrections. They don't wait for the meeting to deal with these matters. This chapter will discuss:

1. Three Best Practices
2. The Review Standards
3. Sitting-in Review Meeting

****

1. Three Best Practices

Reviews are Regular and Rigorous

Review meeting are not designed for enjoyment. They are a candid assessment of performance. If results are good, the review can be quite pleasant. If not, there is nowhere to hide. And for any member of the team who comes unprepared, the review can be painful.

For reviews to be regular and rigorous, the general manager must drive the process. The power must come from the top.

Alamo Tuesday

The management system at the San Antonio operation was as good as any in the country and so were the results. Marvin, the general managers, was the win-ball wizard of the murp, the management review program. He was street-smart, numerate, and singularly obsessive about results. All in all quite a pleasant fellow as long as you delivered.

Time stopped in San Antonio on the second Tuesday of the month. It was a "holy day of obligation." Senior managers blocked that morning on their calendars a year ahead of time. No vacations, no conflicts, no exceptions. The message was clear, be there and be prepared. Three things could happen at a murp. You could come prepared and be on target. You would then be asked to share what you had learned. This was high praise. You could come prepared but with a variance. Even here you had a chance of leaving the room with your head still attached, if you had correctly analyzed the problem and implemented a solution. But you still weren't off the hook.

> "So what I am hearing is that success in this area is influenced by three factors. Fine, so why not develop a contingency plan to deal with them. If you don't have a back-up, you don't have a plan."

And if you had a death-wish you came to the review with a variance and tried to wing it. This was no contest. No one was going to be on target every time, but everyone was expected to analyze the variance and come with a solution.

The senior management murp set the tone for review meetings throughout the organization. They were regular and they were rigorous.

Marvin understood heat as well as light. He was a good problem solver and a good leader. When a problem persisted for a function, he had a habit of showing up unannounced for their weekly review to observe and help out.

"Show and Tell" meetings can be a great complement to review meetings. They focus exclusively on key indicator success stories. Each presenter has no more than 5 minutes and three PowerPoint slides to document his or her success, followed by a question and answer period. The objective is to recognize exceptional performance publicly, to share key learnings and generally to motivate the team. Show and tell meetings are typically conducted on a monthly basis with four or five presenters.

◎ *Reviews are Aligned throughout the Organization.*

When the COBRA system is operating, every level and function has a regular review meeting at a place, time and frequency that best suits the needs of the team. The senior management team may meet in the boardroom once a month. The field sales team may meet weekly at a centrally-located Starbucks with their lap tops. The production shift leaders may conduct a 5 minute end of shift review at a display board next to the line.

It takes a bit of experimentation to determine the right frequency. There are various factors to consider, like the availability of critical information and the ease of getting people together, both your team and your customers. The primary consideration, however, should be the key indicator itself. Each unit manager has to decide how often he or she needs to review an indicator to control it, neither over-controlling nor under-controlling.

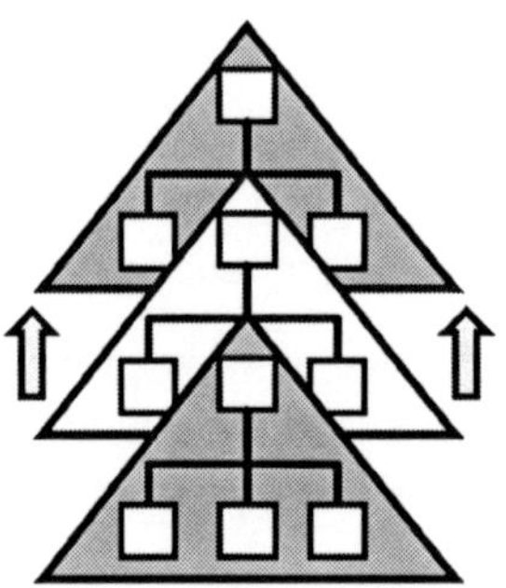

Regional Sales Mgr.

Area Sales Mgr.

Team Leader Mgr.

Ideally, reviews should be sequenced from the ground up within a function. For example, if Team Leaders have weekly team meeting on Friday morning from 8-9 am, then Area Sales Manager should schedule their fortnightly review with all Team Leaders in their area, on the second and fourth Friday of the month at 1pm. This allows Team Leaders to come prepared to the area review with the latest information from their weekly reviews, and so on.

In addition, customers should be present at review meetings whenever customer satisfaction key indicators are discussed. Internal customers are often the next function downstream in the work flow. As illustrated in chart 1, the production unit is the customer of the purchasing unit, and so on. Members of the production team should be present when the purchasing function reviews its customer satisfaction key indicators such as the quality, cost, and timely delivery of raw materials.

Chart 1

Cross-Functional Reviews

Purchasing	*Production*	*Distribution*	*Sales*	*Customer*
Customer: Production ▶	Customer: Distribution ▶	Customer: Sales ▶	Customer: Retailer ▶	Customer: Consumer

The best-run companies align both functional and cross-function review meetings.

 *Balanced Follow-up Occurs*

Balanced measures, soft and hard, require balance follow-up. On-job coaching and review meetings provide this balance.

"Keep your head in the numbers and your feet in the market."

Tore Bu, TCC, Regional Manager, Scandinavia

Coaching enables managers to observe performance first hand—to go and see. Positive results can be recognized and problems can be solved in real time. Review meetings on the other hand enable managers to monitor all the key indicators for the period, to observe trends, and to engage the total team in problem solving—to stop and analyze. The combination of coaching and review provides a balanced picture of what is really happening.

****

2. The Review Standards

The review standards illustrated in chart 2 identify what is required to conduct an effective review meeting. Using these standards, a skilled meeting leader and a prepared team can deal with problems and opportunities as they arise.

Chart 2

		Review Standards
1.	Rules of the Road	Are the rules of the road followed?
2.	Key Indicators	Are targets set for each key indicator for the period?
3.	Tracking	Is the information for the period timely and accurate?
4.	Leadership	Does the meeting leader use the appropriate leadership style?
5.	3 Question Review, Question 1	Is the responsible individual/team held accountable for results?
6.	3 Question Review, Question 2	Is the cause of negative variances identified?
7.	3 Question Review, Question 3	Are solutions found and actions taken?
8.	Get Around Table	Are all key indicators reviewed at the meeting?
9.	Coaching Plan	Are coaching plans developed for skill-based variances?
10.	Recap	Are meeting notes used to follow-up on action points?

The standards provide a structured path for conducting the review, as well as a basis for coaching the meeting leader. Each of the standards will be discussed below:

Review Standard 1: Rules of Road

The rules of the road help manage group dynamics. They identify how people are expected to conduct themselves, what is ok, what is not ok. Since each team has its own history and work habits, there is no one-size-fits-all version. Five to seven rules are optimum; otherwise the group will become "rule bound." Once adopted by the team, the rules become a self-imposed commitment, like a group contract. Everyone agrees to follow them and to hold each other accountable for living them.

For example, if the meeting leader is too dominant and controls the problem solving, the team needs a rule that encourages *shared problem solving*. Team members also need to be strong enough to call "time out" and give the leader feedback when this rule is broken; and the meeting leader needs to be strong enough to accept the feedback as given. Bad habits can be changed quickly when this is done.

A "pro-participation" rule may be needed if some team members remain silent when asked for input or suggestions. Perhaps they are not prepared, perhaps they are timid, or perhaps they are accustomed to coasting along without making much of a contribution. Here a rule like *share your point of view* is needed. In this case, team members need to realize that they have "a seat at the table" because their ideas are valued. They are responsible for under-standing the issues and forming a point of view. It is not ok to remain silent when the team is problem solving. Those that do, are called on it.

At Intel, a closely related rule of the road is: *support your case with facts*. Anyone can challenge anyone else's idea as long as they are prepared to prove it.

"Without data, an idea is only a story, a representation of reality and thus subject to distortion." [1]

The best rules are concrete and observable. If too abstract, they are difficult to observe and therefore to change. Here are some examples of rules of the road used by various teams:

Come Prepared - especially if you have a key indicator with a variance. Identify the probable cause(s) with a fishbone or data analysis of some sort—not just guessing. Have a recommended solution when you walk in the door of a review. If possible, implement the solution beforehand. Other rules might include:

- Be on time
- Talk straight, admit mistakes
- Wave the Flags
- Cell phones off, lap tops down
- One person talks at a time
- Openly confront problems, "Get your Cards on the Table"
- Don't distort or "fiddle" the numbers
- Treat people with respect and dignity
- Recognize positive results

Keep in mind you should restrict your rules to your biggest group dynamics problems and limit those to no more than 5-7 rules at a time.

Teams that use rules of the road most effectively develop them collaboratively and apply them to the behavior of the leader and the team. Rules correct behavior that undermines the meeting. They are not meant to be a list of virtues. Once the problem behavior has been extinguished, they should be changed.

If you keep one eye on the posted rules and the other on the group behavior as it occurs, you can determine if the rules are being followed.

Review Standard 2: Key Indicators

If the 5 component performance management system has been built properly, the key indicators and the standards or goals should be well understood.

Review Standard 3: Tracking System

Again, if the system has been built properly, tracking reports with actual performance versus goal or standards are used.

Review Standard 4: Leadership Effectiveness

We have all been in meetings where the leader was either too dominant or too submissive. As referenced in chart 3 below, review meetings require a range of leadership styles. Meeting leaders must be able to assess quickly the readiness of others and shift styles as needed, moving up or down the steps. The leader needs: to engage the team in problem solving (Style 3&4) when the team can contribute; to give developmental feedback (Style 2) when appropriate; and if readiness is low to take charge (style 1).

Chart 3

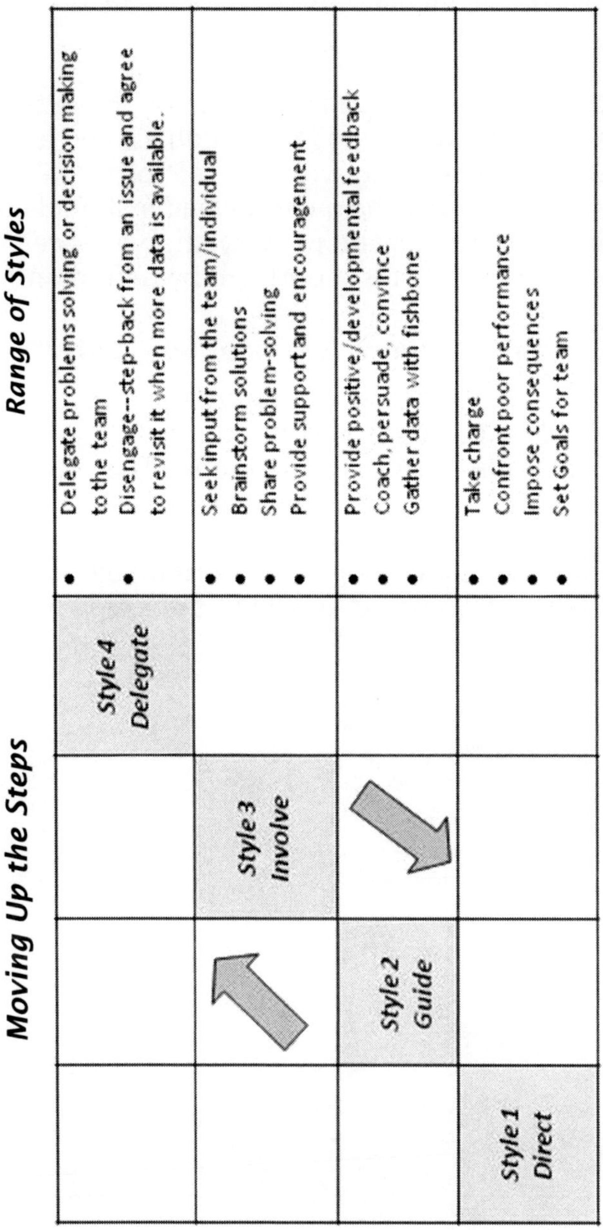

Moving Up the Steps				***Range of Styles***
			Style 4 Delegate	• Delegate problems solving or decision making to the team • Disengage--step-back from an issue and agree to revisit it when more data is available.
		Style 3 Involve		• Seek input from the team/individual • Brainstorm solutions • Share problem-solving • Provide support and encouragement
	Style 2 Guide			• Provide positive/developmental feedback • Coach, persuade, convince • Gather data with fishbone
Style 1 Direct				• Take charge • Confront poor performance • Impose consequences • Set Goals for team

With permission of Keilty, Goldsmith and Company

Review Standard 5: How are you doing compared to target or standard?

This is the first question of the *Three Question Review*. If your management system is working effectively, this question will be easy to answer since you have key indicators, targets, and a tracking system in place to provide data on actual performance.

As illustrated in chart 4, if performance is on or above target, the team leader should provide positive feedback and ask the performer to share key learning with the rest of the team. If performance is below target, the meeting leader should move on to the second review question – why the variance? Any negative variance from target is a problem by definition.

Review Standard 6: "If there is a problem, why?"

If the individual or the team understands the cause of the problem, the second question can be answered quickly. If not, the meeting leader needs to intervene. The Southeast Corner of chart 4 is not an easy place to get out of – a problem exists and the individual or the team does not know why. It is not enough for the leader to just say--bring solutions not problems. The team often needs coaching on how to identify the cause of a problem.

Chart 4

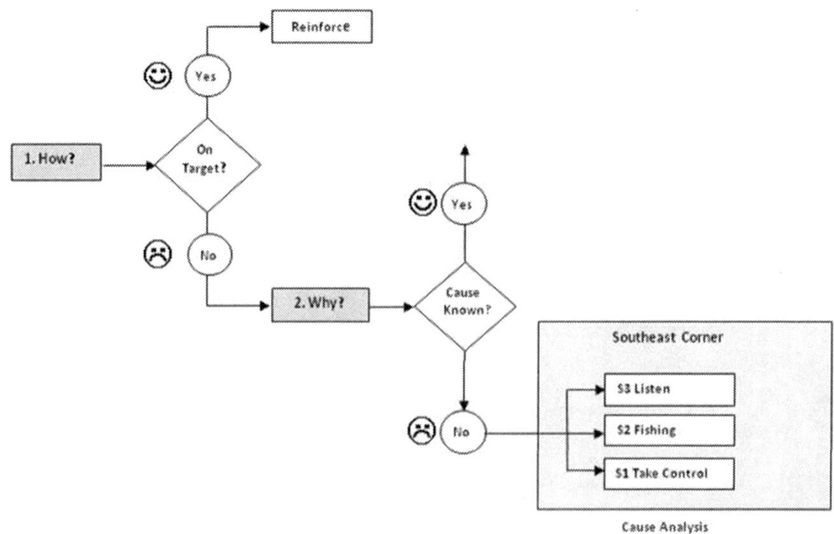

As logical and straight forward as it seems, analyzing the cause of a problem is the most demanding step in the problem solving process.

Sometimes the cause analysis is ignored, and sometimes it is flawed. When a team is struggling with a problem, it is always a relief when someone takes charge. When this happens, however, a warning bell should go off.

"This discussion is over; this is exactly what we are going to do..."

"We're talking this thing to death, here's what we need to do!"

"I realize I've got a problem, but I've got a plan and I am ready to move on it."

What is common about these responses? They are forceful, decisive and focused on solving the problem. What is dangerous about these responses? There is little evidence that the cause of the problem is understood. It is easy to be fooled in a review meeting, by forceful, decisive language. It is more dramatic than cool, probing analysis. Action-heroes seem impressive at first, but colleagues turn skeptical when the same problems keep coming up in one review meeting after another.

Clearly, it is hard to find the solution to a problem if you don't know what is causing it. Here are three approaches to identifying the cause of a problem; each requires a different leadership style. It is best to start with style 3 and shift to style 2 or 1 as required.

Style 3 Listening

This style works best with people who have a fairly good understanding of the problem, but who lack confidence in their problem solving skills. The meeting leader needs to provide encouragement, ask open, "fill in the blank" questions, and listen to the responses. If this is not effective, the leader should move on to style 2.

Style 2 Fishing

Fishing works best with people who are motivated to find a solution but do not know how to identify the cause of the problem. Often they are carrying around a lot of useful information in their head about the cause of the problem, yet they can't process it. Here it is helpful to develop a fishbone diagram as illustrated in chart 5. The fishbone identifies all of the possible causes of a variance. The leader can then ask closed, yes-or-no questions to identify the actual cause. Each bone of the fish requires an answer. Is this a problem?—yes, no, don't know, etc. When a possible cause is eliminated, this should be well reasoned. The individual may not know the exact cause of the variance, but he or she can eliminate some causes and narrow the search.

In many cases the actual cause will emerge from the fishbone exercise. In other cases, more information is needed. If the individual is unwilling to cooperate--blaming others, making excuses, and arguing--it's time for style 1.

Style 1 Taking Control

This style provides clear direction, and is some cases, imposes consequences. When used effectively, Style 1usually causes the performer to become more cooperative and willing to share what he or she knows about the problem, which opens the way to the fishbone diagram.

Fishbone Diagrams

Fishbone diagrams were developed by Ichiro Ishikawa who, along with Edwards Deming, launched the quality movement in Japan. They are a very useful problem-solving tool.

It is not a pretty sight to watch a team try to explain a variance when under pressure and not prepared. This usually triggers an array of unproductive behavior: guessing, blaming, and covering. The fishbone diagram identifies all the possible causes of a problem. Chart 5 is an example of a simple fishbone for troubleshooting a flashlight that won't light. Each of the possible causes must be tested to eliminate non-causes and identify the actual cause of the problem

Chart 5

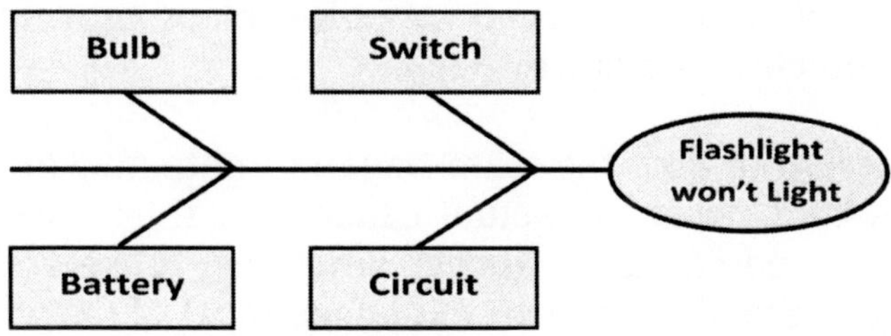

Yes, it is true that some problems can be the result of multiple and intermittent causes. But, try to avoid complicating what is inherently a simple process. The best fishbone diagrams are developed by the team in a brainstorming session. Simply ask the team to identify reasons why a key indicator can be below target and build your fishbone.

Chart 6

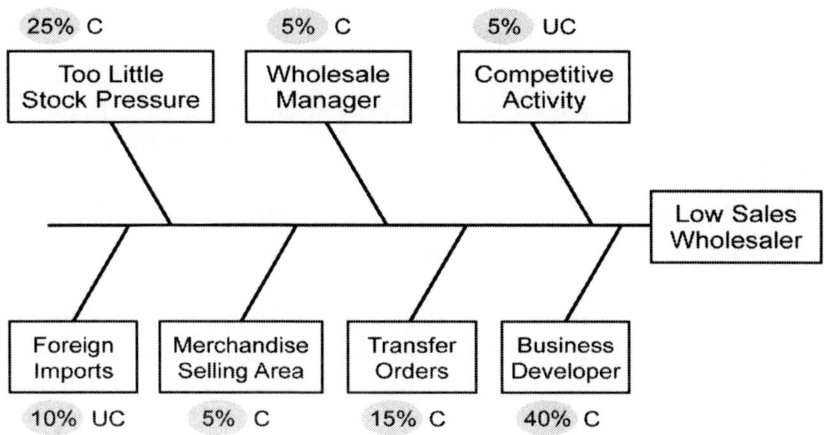

C=controllable, UC=uncontrollable

A Case Study: Sales below Target for a major Beverage Wholesaler

Chart 6 illustrates a fishbone diagram developed by a team of business developers who call on food and beverage wholesalers. The fishbone identifies seven possible causes why sales for the product line could be below target. This fishbone went through several revisions, until the team reached a point where they felt it was good enough to solve most of the problems, most of the time. If sales were below target for the period, they had only to check seven variables, many of which could be done quickly by a store check.

Over a period of time the team began to note how often each potential cause was the actual cause of a sales variance, as seen in the percentages above. What they observed was a familiar pattern; three causes explained most of the variances. Put another way, 80%, or most of the time, one of the following three factors caused the problem:

- *Stock Pressure* -- product available on the shelf or in the back room
- *Transfer orders*-- orders generated by Business Developers calling directly on retail outlets on behalf of the wholesaler.
- *Business Developer*--this had to do with the developer's skill in selling, managing promotions, managing stock taking, and planning deliveries.

In addition, notice that only 15% of the time is the problem outside the control of the sales team: competitive activity and foreign imports. It is fair to say that this key indicator, sales through wholesalers, is controllable by the Business Developer.

It is interesting to note, this example confirms the principle of statistical distribution uncovered in 1906 by Vilfredo Pareto, that clever Italian economist: most effects are the result of a few causes.

Fishbone diagrams not only simplify problem solving, they also help in the planning process by identifying what could go wrong and building in contingencies—what we call "smart fish." When teams have fishbone diagrams for each of their key indicators, problems can be solved immediately rather than waiting for a review meeting. We recommend that teams develop fishbone diagrams for their key indicators, and have them handy on the job as well as displayed at review meeting.

How Time is Spent in a Review

Chart 7 shows the findings of a study we conducted that measured the time spent answering the three review questions. Teams that came prepared spent half the time identifying the cause of a variance (the "why" question), than those that were not prepared.

Chart 7

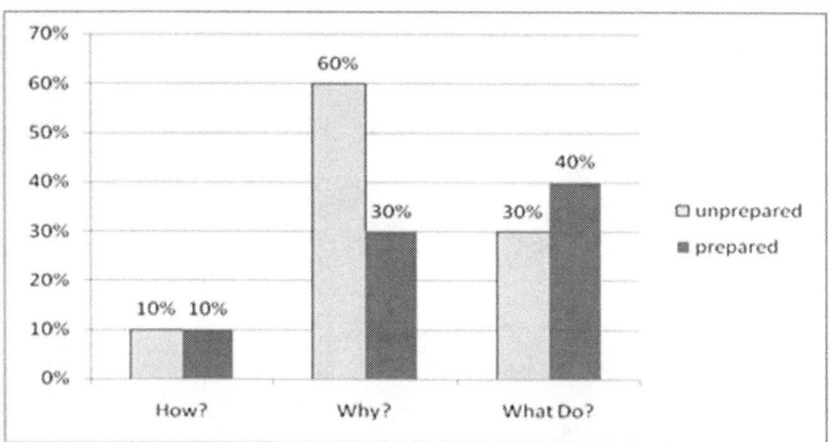

The faster problem solving teams had several things in common. They had an explicit rule of the road about coming prepared. They used a fishbone diagram and a one page fact sheet to "prove the cause" of a variance. And they were ready to recommend alternative solutions. As you will note, they were able to spend less time on causes and more time on finding the best solutions. In most cases the total time of the meeting was shorter as well.

Review Standard 7: What are you doing about the problem?"

This is the third question of the *Three Question Review.* Once you have correctly answered question 2 and understand the cause of the problem, it is time to find a solution. As illustrated in chart 8 in some cases the solution may be obvious once the cause is known. In other cases, the team lacks the readiness to solve the problem, and the meeting leader is pulled into the Southeast Corner.

Chart 8

Three Question Review

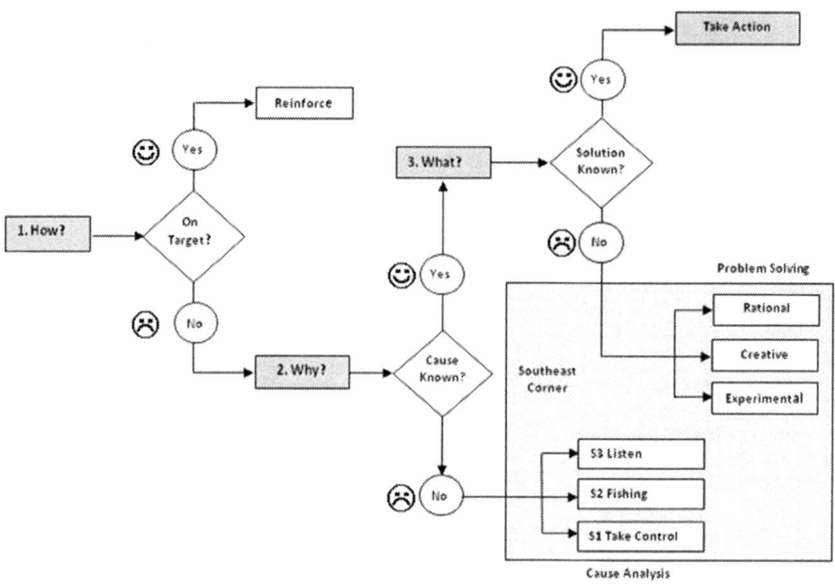

You will recall from our discussion of strategy that there are three planning styles.[2] They are also useful in problem solving and getting out of the Southeast Corner:

Rational Problem Solving

Here, you reason your way to a solution using sound logic and a rigorous examination of the facts. This is appropriate when the cause is known, and data is available to determine the pluses and minuses of various alternatives. It is up to the meeting leader to guide the team to a logical solution.

Creative Problem Solving

As George Prince notes: "*When solutions depend on connections yet to be made, logic must fail.*" [3] With certain problems, data and logic aren't enough. When repeated efforts to reason your way to a solution fail, it is time to get outside the box. Rather than focusing on correcting the current problem, start over with a blank sheet of paper. Structural tension discussed in chapter 6 is an example of a creative problem solving method. Chart 9 identifies some of the differences between rational and creative problems solving:

Chart 9

Rational Problem Solving	***Creative Problem Solving***
Lights on	Lights off
Trouble Shooting a system or process that has been productive in the past.	Something that hasn't been done before
Analysis: Breaking things into component parts	Synthesis: Combining diverse parts in new ways.
Logical: cause/effect relationships	Non-logical: random, intuitive
Linear: one item of knowledge leads to another	Lateral: goes outside the 'obvious' line of thought
Convergent: separates essentials from mass of information; screens out irrelevant data	Divergent: expands the problem and areas for solution
Deductive: makes inferences from available data	Intuitive: jumps to conclusions without proof
Tools	
• Formal Planning/Forecasting	• Visioning
• Logic Tree	• Brainstorming
• Process Mapping/ Fishbone Diagrams	• Lateral Thinking

Experimental Problem Solving

Sometimes you just get bogged-down in solving a problem-- neither a rational, nor a creative style yield a ready solution. You may be considering several options, but no one can make an ironclad case for one or the other. At this point, you usually learn more by trial and error than by further analysis.

Rational problem solving is often referred to as: ready-aim-fire, or analyze-plan-act. At its worst it becomes ready-aim-aim-aim, or analysis-paralysis. Trial and error problem solving is more like ready-fire-aim. When the analysis becomes too messy, stop analyzing - take action, learn by doing, and then refine your plan. Clearly it takes practice to know which of these three problem solving styles or combinations is most appropriate for the problem at hand.

In summary, the *Three Question Review* keeps the review meeting on track, whether it is in the boardroom or the shop floor. Many organizations post chart 8 on the wall of the meeting room as a ready reminder and reference. Now let's discuss the last three standards of an effective review meeting.

Review Standard 8: Getting Around the Table

The objective of the meeting is to review/evaluate all the key indicators for the performance period in the time allotted—to get around the table. For this to happen, everyone must come prepared, and the meeting leader must excel in managing time. If the team gets stuck on one issue, they may not get around the table. On the other hand, finishing the meeting on time should not supersede quality problem solving. If a problem is complex and/or readiness to deal with it is low, it should be tabled until later in the day.

Review Standard 9: Is On-Job Coaching Planned and Reviewed?

The management review provides a great opportunity to identify coaching needs. Skill deficiency can be a factor in any performance problem. It should be one of the bones on every fishbone diagram.

When a skill deficiency is the cause of a problem, a coaching plan should be developed.

As you know by now, we call this *Coaching Against a Variance*, and it follows a 3-week cycle:

- Week 1—a coaching need is identified and coaching is planned for next week.
- Week 2—coaching is conducted
- Week 3—the key indicator is reviewed with the expectation that the variance will be reduced or eliminated.

With this approach, both the coach and the performer are held accountable for measurable performance improvements in the short term. Coaching is no longer ad hoc and informal. Plans are posted and improvements are closely monitored.

Review Standard 10: Meeting Recap

The recap records the key action points of the meeting. Chart 10 is an example of a recap, a simple one page document. The meeting leader completes the recap during the meeting. To insure there is no confusion on the follow-up, the recap is e-mailed to team members.

Chart 10

Review Recap					
Unit: Fleet	*Unit Manager: Ivan Popov*				*Date: 3/21/06*
Who attended review:	*All 4 fleet supervisors*				
Key Indicator	*Std.*	*Actual*	*Neg. Var.*	*Cause*	*Solution/Action Point*
transport maintenance & repair cost per ph/c	0.12	0.12	--		
Fuel usage per 100 km	5.3	7.0	1.6	Poor route planning	Create new routes
Fleet Readiness	97%	85%	12%	Out of stock repair parts	Coach on inventory mgmt. , Tues. AM

At the beginning of each review meeting, the recap from the previous meeting is discussed to ensure that action points have been implemented.

In summary, the ten review standards include the skills and practices needed to conduct an effective review meeting. They provide a structure for conducting the meeting, and a checklist for evaluating the effectiveness of the review.

****

3. Sitting-in Review Meetings

This is a great way to train new managers and to help experienced managers with recurring performance problems. The objective is to help meeting leaders master the review standards. A Review Standards Checklist can be found in the appendix.

There is no faster or better way to determine if a team is managing performance effectively than to sit-in their review meeting.

Sitting-in reviews also is a great way for managers to stay in touch with the teams that report to them. This can occur on a planned or random basis. If performance is good, the positive feedback will be welcomed. If there are unresolved problems, the coaching will be appreciated.

The following suggestions maybe helpful for a manager sitting-in on a review:

- Sit quietly in the back of the meeting room and observe.
- Only intervene during the review if a major problem is not being resolved.
- Use the Review Standards Checklist to record your observations.
- Provide one-on-one feedback to the meeting leader after the meeting.

Chapter Summary

The review meeting is the nerve center of the performance management system. It is a regular, face-to-face meeting to monitor key indicators, analyze variances, and implement solutions. It is the most important meeting any team can have.

Review meetings should be regular and rigorous; they need to be aligned within and across functions; and they must be combined with on-job coaching to achieve balanced follow-up. The tools discussed in this chapter can help develop an effective review process throughout your company.

Now, it's time to get started on aligning your organization with your strategy -- and our concluding chapter will put you on course.

Chapter 11
Getting COBRA Going

Companies that master the COBRA process, out-execute their competitors in the here and now, and stay ahead of them in the future. They continuously test the alignment of both their strategy and their organization and make the necessary changes.

This chapter will discuss how to get COBRA process going in your company:

- Aligning the Strategy with the Business Environment
- Assessing the Alignment of the Organization
- Executing the Change Agenda

Chart 1

The COBRA Alignment Process

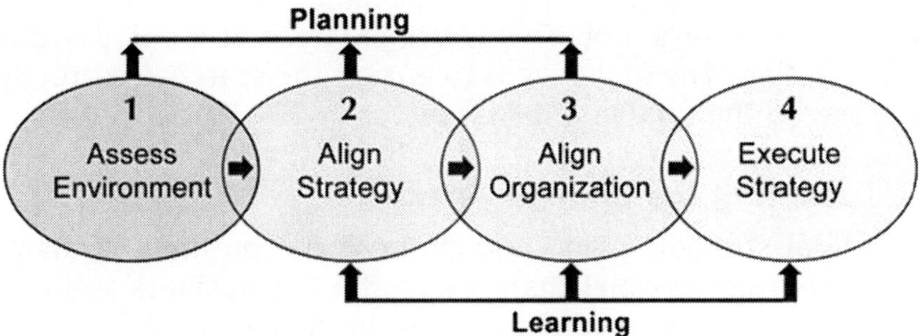

1. Aligning the Strategy with the Business Environment

Assessing the environment and aligning the strategy are the critical first steps in exploiting market opportunities. This is an outside-in proposition, discussed extensively in chapter 6.

There is an array of time-tested, analytic models to guide the alignment of strategy:

- Decision Scenarios
- Competitive Industry Analysis
- Lean Manufacturing
- Portfolio Analysis
- Product Life Cycle Analysis
- Overhead Value Analysis

2. Assessing the Alignment of the Organization

Once the strategic plan is drafted, it is time to determine if the current organization can in fact execute the strategy. This is an inside-out proposition. As we have discussed, when the organization cannot execute the strategy, three factors explain most of the problems most of the time: the structure, the system and the culture--the *Three Points of Pressure*.

COBRA-Scan is designed to assess the alignment of the *Three Points of Pressure*. Tools and processes for conducting the scan were discussed in chapter 6. The scan is normally conducted by a joint client-consultant team. The data gathering rarely takes more than five to seven days at the pilot location. The findings of the scan are shared with the managers and employees of the pilot business unit. This is usually done at a one day off-site meeting. The objective is to ensure the scan has correctly uncovered the fundamental issues.

3. Executing the Change Agenda

The final strategic plan contains both the business strategy and the organizational change agenda. The business strategy identifies what is needed to grow the business. The change agenda identifies the organizational changes that are needed to grow the business.

In-Flight Redesign

Execution, for most of the 20th century, involved optimizing performance with the current organization. Execution, in the 21st century, involves transforming the current organization in order to optimize performance. Everyone onboard has a role to play.

The remainder of this chapter will focus on how to execute the change agenda. Changing the organization involves changing embedded roles, values, and work habits. This kind of change takes people out of their comfort zone. If they don't understand why change is necessary, it is natural for them to resist.

Therefore, it is especially important that all levels of the organization are involved in the realignment process. The scan seeks their input in identifying alignment issues. The data-sharing helps clarify the issues and build a commitment to the change agenda.

Program Approach Vs Business-Unit Approach

In this section we will discuss two ways to execute the change agenda: the program approach and the business-unit approach. They can be used separately or in combination. The merits of each are discussed below.

Program Approach

As discussed in chapter 2, a variety of programs have been used to implement organizational change: Reengineering, Total Quality Management, Six Sigma, Participative Management, Competency-Based Development and so on.

Programs are usually implemented from the top-down, throughout the total company. They involve off-site and classroom training sessions that provide participants with the concepts and skills to implement change back on the job. Programs can be quite effective in changing individual skills and attitudes. However, by attempting to change the total company at one time they can also be risky, especially when the inevitable resistance sets-in.

Business-Unit Approach

Here the focus is on a direct, hands-on change of a specific business unit rather than the total company. The change is encouraged but not mandated from the top. The responsibility for implementing change rests squarely on the shoulders of the business unit (note: *Putting it All Together: Case 2 below).* Strategic business objectives are agreed to by the unit. They are nonnegotiable. It is up to the business-unit team to decide if they need to change the organization in order to achieve these objectives. Corporate support for change is available upon request. This is a voluntary, self-determined approach to realigning the organization.

We have learned from experience that the business-unit approach usually works best. In their study of corporate renewal, Michael Beers and his colleagues also found this to be true:

> ***"Starting corporate renewal at the very top is a high-risk revitalization strategy not employed by the most successful companies. Organizations should start corporate revitalization by targeting small operations...not large, central, core operations."*** [1]

Convincing clients of this is a challenge. They understandably want to implement change as quickly as possible, and feel the best way to do so is with a top-down program, implemented across the total company.

In implementing the business-unit approach, we select a single business unit that is ready and willing to pilot the change. Though limited in scope, the pilot enables us to build a working model and move up the learning curve. Once the pilot is up and running, other business units are invited to visit the pilot operation and observe the changes first hand. This helps dispel unwarranted fears and reduce the resistance to change.

Now the change effort is accelerated. After observing the benefits of the pilot, multiple business-units typically volunteer to implement the change concurrently. While program change is a top-down affair, business-unit change is more centrifugal, spreading outward across the organization from a successful pilot.

In the long run business-unit change has proven to be quicker and more effective than program change.

****

Executing the Change Agenda: Case 1

What follows is a 4 phase change agenda which deals with the most common alignment problems uncovered in COBRA-scans with clients. As seen in chart 2, these problems create a segmented organization. We have experimented with various ways to sequence these interventions and have found the four phase agenda generally works best.

Chart 2

	Key Scan Findings:		
	1. Culture	***2. Structure***	***3. System***
Segmented Org.	There is no shared vision of where the company is headed. The values of teamwork and customer service need to be established. Managers and supervisors need to improve their leadership and analytical skills to more effectively operate the system at their level.	Major boundaries between functions are undermining productivity and customer satisfaction.	The system is effective within functions but not across functions. Key indicators focus only on functional performance. Cross-function review meetings do not occur.

Phase 1: Realigning the Culture

Several cultural change interventions discussed in chapter 3 are initiated in this phase. A team of senior managers is formed to define the company's vision and to articulate the values of teamwork and customer service. It generally takes 2 months to define the vision and values and to get them communicated throughout the organization. To be internalized, they need to be regularly modeled and reinforces back on the job. This is usually a company-wide intervention.

Peer-based feedback, or 360˚ feedback, is generally introduced at this time as well. It provides confidential feedback to leaders at every level, on how satisfied their co-workers are with their day-to-day leadership practices and the way they live the values.

Managers and supervisors of the pilot business unit also receive leadership and analytical problem-solving training.

Phase 2: Realigning the Structure

In both phase 2 and 3 the change agenda is implemented in a pilot business unit. Phase 2 starts with the Customer Maps & Mission intervention discussed in chapter 4. Customer maps identify the internal or final customer of each function, and the products or services it provides to each customer. The mission explicitly defines cross-functional roles and responsibilities. This builds-on and reinforces the values of teamwork and customer service introduced in phase 1. The train-do-review-install change cycle discussed below is used to implement this intervention.

The cultural norms of leading-up and leading-across discussed in chapter 3 are also introduced in phase 2. It generally takes one month to implement phase 2 interventions. In some cases phase 1 and 2 are implemented concurrently.

Phase 3: Realigning the System

To be effective, the system needs to operate across all levels and functions of a business unit. The boundary management interventions in phase 2 define the roles and relationship needed to manage across boundaries. This sets the stage for realigning the system.

The scan findings in chart 2 indicate that key indicators and review meetings are overly focused on functional performance. Customer satisfaction key indicators do not exist; and cross-functional review meetings do not occur. This fosters disruptive boundaries between functions which cripple execution.

In this case, the system interventions involve two modules: realigning key indicators and x-functional review meetings. Chart 3 illustrates the change cycle used to implement these modules. It is a hybrid of the program and business-unit approach. The 'do-review' elements put structure and accountability into the change process.

Chart 3

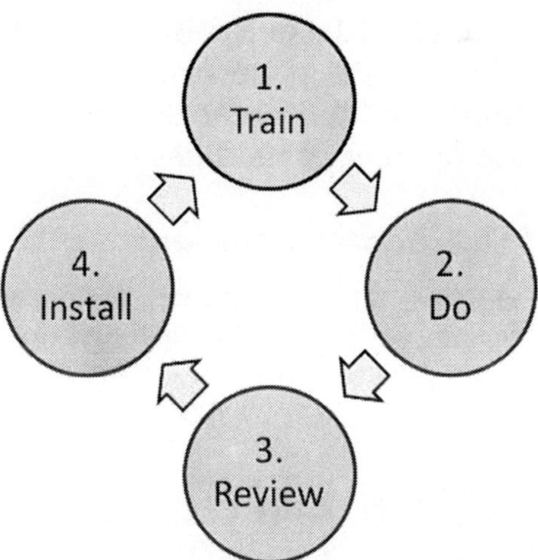

- *Train*: The first module deals with realigning key indicators. The training includes the skills, tools and processes discussed in chapter 7. All teams leave the training session with the assignment of realigning their key indicators.

- *Do*: Each team is given 2-3 weeks to *do*, or complete, the assignment, which involves identifying functional, customer satisfaction and execution key indicators. This entails working closely with one's functional team as well as with one's internal or final customers. Internal organizational development (OD) specialists support each team.

- *Review*: Each team presents their realigned key indicators to the president of the business unit and the COBRA consultant. This is a go/no-go review. If the assignment is incorrect, it is reworked in short order.

- *Install*: Once the key indicators for all the teams are reviewed and approved, the changes are installed and become operational. There are few problems with transfer of learning.

Each module is sequenced in a logical manner; each lays the foundation for the next.

When the first module is installed by all functions, we move on to the second module. It generally takes approximately three to four months to implement the phase 3 interventions depending on the number of modules.

Phase 4: Roll-Out Across Company

As discussed earlier, at this point the change effort is accelerated. After observing the benefits of the pilot, multiple business-units typically volunteer to implement the change concurrently.

Putting it All Together: Case1

To summarize, implementing the first three phases of the change agenda takes approximately 4-6 months. As noted in chart 4, the *Three Points of Pressure* are highly interdependent.

Chart 4

	Key Scan Findings		
	Phase 1: Culture	***Phase 2: Structure***	***Phase 3: System***
Segment-ed Org.	There is no shared vision of where the company is headed. The values of teamwork and customer service need to be established. Managers and supervisors need to improve their leadership and analytical skills to more effectively operate the system at their level.	Major boundaries between functions are undermining systems productivity and customer satisfaction.	System is effective within functions but not across functions. Key indicators focus only on functional performance. Cross-function review meetings do not occur.
Change Interven-tions	**Vision, Values & Skills:** • Define Corporate Vision & values • Build necessary leadership and mgmt. competencies	**Maps & Missions:** Define the roles and responsibilities of each function: • Functional Work • X-Functional work	**Measures & Reviews:** Establish performance measures and accountability for cross-functional work
Aligned Org.	Vision builds a unity of purpose. The values of teamwork and customer service help resolve boundary conflicts. Managers at all levels have the leadership and mgmt. skills to operate the system at their level.	Maps & Missions define: • Internal & Final Customers • Role of Supplier • Role of Customer • Working relations	Each function measures internal productivity and customer satisfaction. Regular functional and X-functional review meetings occur.

Building vision, values and skills (phase 1) and clarifying functional maps and missions (phase 2) are necessary but not sufficient to realign the organization. These interventions can quickly fade away, if the management system remains unchanged.

With an aligned system (phase 3), each function sets targets for internal productivity as well as customer satisfaction, and monitors and reviews these targets on a regular basis. The structural and cultural interventions set in motion changes that support the system interventions. All three are needed to achieve lasting change. Over time, changes to the structure and the system become embedded in the culture.

Executing the Change Agenda: Case 2

The following is an example of realigning just one function in and otherwise highly effective business unit. It took two months to create the problem and six months to solve it. A combination of the business-unit and the program approach were employed. Each module was implemented using the train-do-review-install change cycle.

The Ice Palace at Full Moon

Weather Report: Wind Chill: -40 ° F, 6-7" of Snow, Moon Phase: Full

At last the numbers where moving in the right direction; her customers were delighted; her team was motivated--and Galina's smile filled the sky.

The last eight months had been horrible. In May, Galina Rogozina had been promoted to manager of the Order Entry unit in St. Petersburg, Russia. She was clearly the most qualified candidate. However she was also a good friend of the departing supervisor who had appointed her. Most of the seasoned members of the unit felt they should have been appointed and left the company. As turnover soared, so did operator errors. The unit's seven internal customers--Sales, Delivery, Finance, Warehouse, Marketing, HR, and Procurement--were very unhappy with the dramatic decline in service.

There was nothing faint-hearted about Galena. She dug-in and worked longer and harder to rebuild the team. As they moved into peak season and the work-load continued to increase, the unit hit the wall. Internal customers were hostile and the final retail customers were switching to the competition. Most of the order entry operators were new and overwhelmed.

Finally In July Galina gave Elena, the COBRA Coordinator, a call. They jointly assessed the effectiveness of the team, and put a plan together. It was time to hit the "reset button".

They started with the Maps and Mission intervention. The order entry team sat down with each of their seven customers and listened to their requirements and discussed ways to correct operator errors. Though often painful, these face-to-face meetings served to clarify the unit's mission in concrete terms. They then moved on to identify internal and customer satisfaction key indicators. These were reviewed with the team on a daily basis, and with customers on a weekly basis.

Once the structure and the system were running smoothly, Elena conducted several off-site meetings to further develop teamwork and customer service skills. By October turnover was down to zero and operator errors were starting to decline. The final COBRA intervention was an on-job coaching module, since many of the customer errors were caused by unskilled operators.

By January operator errors had dropped by 70%, much like the temperature, and yes Galina's smile shone like the ice palace at full moon.

Putting Organizational Alignment on the Dashboard

Chart 5 illustrates the findings of an initial COBRA-Scan survey conducted with a client in March and a second survey conducted in December of the same year. It monitors the improvements in the performance management system and in customer service.

Chart 5

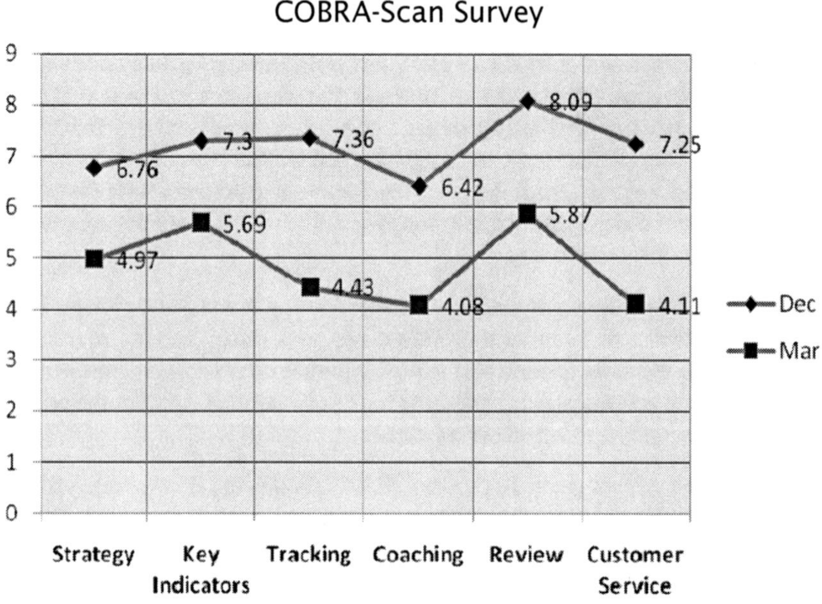

The four phase change agenda discussed earlier was implemented in this operation after the initial scan in March. By December there had been a twenty percent gain in performance across the board, which is always the acid test of a change intervention. In this company, organizational alignment became a closely-watched, key indicator that was regularly monitored and managed.

Summary of the Book

Companies that prosper in turbulent times are strategically agile in identifying opportunities, and organizationally agile in exploiting them. Getting the strategy right is more important than ever. Yet it is not enough, if it can't be executed. This book is based on the premise that execution matters as much or more than strategy in a global environment.

COBRA is an early warning and response system that keeps the organization aligned with the realities of the business environment—so that strategy can be executed. A company's execution capability, its ExCap, is a function of the leader's skill (L) in aligning the structure, the system and the culture.

ExCap = L x (Structure + System + Culture)

Chapters 2-5 provide tools for aligning these critical factors; chapters 6-10 provide additional tools for aligning the five components of the performance management system; and this chapter provides tools for implementing the changes that are needed to realign the organization with the strategy. To make it happen!

COBRA is the X factor in strategy execution. Leaders that master the alignment process can execute their strategy today, and stay ahead of their competitors in executing their strategy in the future. They have the capacity to effect renewal and sustain growth.

Notes

Chapter 1

1. Larry Bossidy & Ram Charan, *Execution, The Discipline of Getting Things Done*, Crown Business, 2002.

Chapter 2

1. Michael L. Dertouzos, et.al. *Made in America: Regaining the Productive Edge*, MIT Commission on Industrial Productivity, HarperPerennial,1989.
2. Peter F. Drucker, *Managing in Turbulent Times*, Harper & Row Publishers,1980.
3. Richard Tanner Pascale, *Managing on the Edge, A Touchstone Book*, Published by Simon & Schuster Inc. 1980, New York. Reprinted by permission of International Creative Management, Inc. © *Copyright 1990 by Richard Pascale*
4. Paul R. Lawrence & Jay W. Lorsch, *Organization and Environment*, Harvard Business School Press, 1986.
5. Rosabeth Moss Kanter, *The Change Masters*, Simon & Schuster, New York, 1983.
6. John P. Kotter, *Organizational Dynamics: Diagnosis and Intervention*, Addison-Wesley, 1978.
7. Richard Pascale and Anthony Athos, *The Art of Japanese Management*, Warner Books, 1982.
8. David Hanna, *Designing Organizations for High Performance*, Addison-Wesley, 1988.
9. G.Fuchberg, "Quality Programs Show Shoddy Results," The Wall Street Journal, May 14, 1992, sec. B.
10. Michael Beer, Russell A. Eisenstat and Bert Spector, *The Critical Path to Corporate Renewal*, Harvard Business School Press, 1990.

Chapter 3

1. William E. Schneider, *The Re-engineering Alternative*, Irwin Professional Publishing, 1994
2. John P. Kotter and James L Heskett, *Corporate Culture and Performance*, Free Press, 1992

3. James C. Collins & Jerry I. Porras, *Built to Last Successful Habits of Visionary Companies*, Harper Business, 1994
4. *Made in America: Regaining the Productive Edge*, MIT Commission on Industrial Productivity
5. Judith M. Bardwick, *Danger in the Comfort Zone*, American Management Association, 1995.
6. James G. March, "Exploration and Exploitation in Organizational Learning", Organizational Science, 2 (1991) 71-87.
7. Jim Collins, *Good to Great...Why Some Companies Make the Leap and Others Don't*, HarperCollinsPublishers, 2001.
8. Jeffrey K. Liker, *The Toyota Way*, McGraw-Hill, 2004.

Chapter 4

1. Richard J. Schonberger, *Building a Chain of Customers*, Hutchinson Business Books, 1990.
2. Willaim A.Pasmore & John J. Sherwood, *Sociotechnical Systems: A Sourcebook*, University Associates, Inc.,1978
3. Edward Lawler III, *High-Performance Management*, Jossey-Bass Publishers, 1986.
4. Mina Kimes, Cisco Systems Layers It On, Fortune Dec 8th, 2008.
5. Jay R. Galbraith, *Organizational Design*, Addison-Wesley, 1997.
6. Geary A. Rummler & Alan P. Brache, *Improving Performance: How to Manage the White Space on the Organization Chart*, Jossey-Bass, San Francisco, 1990.
7. "Increasing Customer Satisfaction through Effective Complaint Handling", TARP Worldwide, 2005.

Chapter 5

1. Michael C. Mankins & Richard Steele, Turning Great Strategy into Great Performance, Harvard Business Review, July-August 2005, Vol. 83, issue 7/8.
2. Jon R. Katzenbach & Douglas K. Smith, *The Wisdom of Teams*, Harvard Business School Press, 1993.

Chapter 6

1. Tech>Mark Consulting Group, *Management Vision*, 1988, pg 24.
2. Patricia Jones & Larry Kahaner, *Say It and Live It: The 50 Corporate Mission Statements That Hit the Mark*, New York: Doubleday, 1955.
3. From: Atlanta Journal-Constitution (Oct 21, 2007).
4. Henry Mintzberg, *Managers, Not MBAs ... A hard look at the soft practice of managing and management development*, Berrett-Koehler, San Francisco, 2004.
5. James C. Collins & Jerry I. Porras, *Built to Last: Successful Habits of Visionaty Companies*, Harper Business, 1994.
6. Jason Jennings & Laurence Naughton, *It's Not the Big that Eat the Small ... It's the Fast that Eat the Slow*, Harper Business, 2002.
7. Robert Fritz, *The Path of Least Resistance for Managers*, Berrett-Koehler Publishers, Inc. 1999.
8. Pierre Wack, *Scenarios: Uncharted Water Ahead, HBR, Strategy, Seeking and Securing Competitive Advantage*, edited by Cynthia A. Montgomery and Michael E. Porter.
9. Michael Porter, The Five Forces that Shape Strategy,HBR,Jan 2008, 79-93.
10. Donald R. Lehmann & Russell S. Winer, *Analysis for Marketing Planning*, 6th ed. (Boston: McGraw-Hill/Irwin, 2005).
11. Richard Tedlow, *The Education of Andy Grove*, Fortune, December 12, 2005, pg 122.
12. Interview with Jim Stuart, Marketing Director, Consolidate Coca-Cola Bottling Company.

Chapter 7

1. The Economist Intelligence Unit, #8173711137, *A New Look at Corporate Performance Measurements*.
2. George L. Morrisey, *Management by Objectives and Results for Business and Industry*, Addison-Wesley, 1970.
3. Jeffrey K. Liker, *The Toyota Way*, McGraw-Hill, 2004.
4. Pat Kerwin, National Football League Analyst, Sirius Radio
5. Gary L. Neilson, Karla L. Martin, & Elisabeth Powers, Harvard Business Review, June 2008.

Chapter 8

1. Thomas L. Friedman, *The Lexus and the Olive Tree*, Anchor Books, 2000.
2. Source: United Parcel Service
3. Dan Strata, Why Today's IT Organizations Won't Work Tomorrow, A.T. Kearney Study taken from The Cart Pulling the Horse?, Economist, Apr 7, 2005.
4. Mary Walton, *The Deming Management Method*, Dodd, Mead & Company, 1986
5. Gary Walters, Selection Chairman for NCAA Basketball Tournament., USA TODAY, March 13, 2007.
6. Mary Walton, *The Deming Management Method*, Dodd, Mead & Company, 1986.

Chapter 9

1. Larry Bossidy & Ram Charan, *Execution, the Discipline of Getting Things Done*, CrownBusiness, 2002.
2. Jack Welch with Suzy Welch, *Winning*, New York: Harper Business, 2005
3. Fred E. Fiedler, *A Theory of Leadership Effectiveness*. New York: McGraw-Hill, 1967.
4. Paul Hersey and Kenneth H. Blanchard, *Management of Organizational Behavior*, Prentice Hall, Englewood Cliffs, New Jersey. 1969

Chapter 10

1. Richard S. Tedlow, Fortune Dec, 12, 2005, pg138
2. Henry Mintzberg, *Managers, Not MBAs...a hard look at the soft practices of managing and management development*, Berrett-Koehler, San Francisco, 2004.
3. George Prince,*The Practice of Creativity*, Collier Books, Div. of Macmillion Publishing, Co. Inc., New York, 1970.

Chapter 11

1. Michael Beer, Russell A. Eisenstat, Bert Spector, *The Critical Path to Corporate Renewal*, Harvard Business School Press, 1990.

Acknowledgements

Designing the cover of this book was a welcome closure to a long journey. Yet, when it came to putting my name on the cover, it didn't feel quite right. The concepts and best practices that are shared in this book come from many sources: some from the enduring management science models, most from lessons-learned with our clients.

1978 to 1981

During this period I was fortunate to be on a team that developed a management system for the U.S. Bottlers of Coca-Cola. It was called Total Management Impact (TMI) and was designed around the best management practices of our best bottlers. I want to thank the many bottlers that contributed to this program, and the many bottlers that successfully implemented it. I also want to thank the members of our team: Marvin Griffin, Don Ulrich, Gene Richardson, Bill Atchison and Ron Elrod. I learned from all of you. Many of the TMI fundamentals found their way into the COBRA design.

1981-1986

From 1981-1986 I worked for the Northern European Division of The Coca-Cola Company. Here again I want to thank the bottlers from the seven countries of our division. Together we developed and implemented many interventions to improve strategy execution. For their many contributions I would like to thank: John O'Connell, Tom O'Beirne, Alfie Lydon, Jack Holt, Leo Creery, John Barrett, Harry Hamilton, Eddie Campbell, Adrian McGarry, Wim Junge, Tora Bu, Wayne Jones, Greg Sand and Ron Read. Many of these learnings became elements of the COBRA design.

1986-1994

In 1986 I joined Keilty, Goldsmith and Boone (KGB), a management consulting firm that specialized in leadership and organizational change. From my partners in the KGB, I learned the theory and practice of leadership and team building. I also continued to help clients improve their strategy execution. These learnings, along with what I had learned working with bottlers, became the genesis of COBRA. It was first piloted in Argentina in 1992 with the Buenos Aires Bottler. I would like to thank Luis Arzeno, Barksdale Collins, Buddy Buchanan, and all the managers and supervisor from that operation for making the pilot a success. We learned a lot from the pilot that helped us improve the COBRA design.

Later that year COBRA was piloted in the Athens's operation of the Hellenic Bottling Company (HBC). For their many contributions in implementing COBRA throughout the Greek operation, I want to thank: Dr. Gerry Reidy, Tito Kominos, John Androutsopoulos, Nick Androutsopoulos, Doros Contantinou, Tom Poulos, Diamantes Niccolaou, Constantinos Sfakakis, Kleon Yavassoglou, Stratos Volanis, Vicky Tatas, and Chrisilla Bakea. And a very special thanks to Nikos Mirmiroglou for his relentless effort in implementing COBRA in Greece and in the many countries of HBC. He was the good cop on our team.

1994 to 2006

During this period COBRA was implemented in most of the 28 countries of HBC as well as with other clients. I want to thank all the fine managers and supervisors that implemented COBRA into their operation throughout HBC. We again learned new and better practices that became part of the COBRA design. Special thanks go out to: Irial Finan, Tony Maher, Cynthia McCague, Syd Farley, Libby McKnight, Richard Abbey, Ian Murdock, Pat Paya, Damien Gammell, John Wier, Frank O'Donnell, Marcel Martin, Ovidiu Burlacu, Mircea Draja, Baring Olafsson, Paul Mulligan, Tudor Bourgachiehf, Mila Stoytcheva, Elena Shestakova, Victoria Sidyakima, Nikolay Kholodin, Anna Shamanova, Dimitri Mackavos, Dieter Moser, Clemens Spechtler, Stanislav Antos, Petra Tomanek, Steven Lusk, Pericles Venieres, and Wojciech Turski. Elena Shestakova deserves special praise for her tireless efforts in implementing COBRA across the vast Russian market, as well as to Klaus Farfsing who implement COBRA in various Central European countries.

COBRA was also introduced to the AMATIL Bottler in Australia and New Zealand. Here again I want to thank: Warrick White, Jon Scriven, Dean Brennan, and George Adams. We learned many best practices from this excellent operation.

2007--2008

In February 2007 I started writing this book. Again I have many people to thank. Some from the beverage industry: John Hunter, Gerry Reidy, Tom O'Beirne, Norb Cole, John Walter, Dan Haas, Tom Carney, Ben Knight , Sandy McDonald, Gordie Wilkinson, Leonard Kowalewski, and Jim Stuart. Others that provided help came from a broad range of industries: Christos Tsolkas, Judith Bardwick, Rob Bond, Daniel Carlson, George Gaxiola, Cliff Thompson, Vernon Sanders, John Nixon, Meg Burns, Sam Janetta, Ben Blount, Bud Wright, Don Perozzi, Frank Wagner, Jerry Gardner and Professor Bobby Friedman. All were very generous with their time and their feedback. All helped me organize and simplify my writing.

Special praise for assistance above and beyond the call of duty goes out to Tom O'Beirne, John Walter, and Professor Bobby Friedman. Tom helped edited the first draft of the book in Dún Laoghaire, Ireland...with only an occasional break for a stroll down to the local pub for a Guinness. Tom has run bottling operations around the world and helped me keep things short and simple. John Walter is the archetype road-warrior, having managed Coca-Cola operations in the Philippines, Australia, Japan, Argentina, Peru, Bolivia, Chile, Colombia, Ecuador, and Venezuela. He has been a constant companion, reviewing and editing countless rewrites. He was particularly helpful in developing chapter 6 on strategic planning. Bobby Friedmann, a Marketing Professor at the Terry College of Business, University of Georgia, also helped review and edit numerous rewrites of the book. He also encouraged me to make my case with anecdotes and best practices from the field.

I would also like to thank Lea Agnew for her fine editing job and Michael Alderman for all her help on the graphics. And of course a hug and a kiss to my loving and tolerant wife. She knew when to tip toe around my office when I was in a writer's funk--and when to kick the door down when her honey-do list got too long. Bless you. And finally I would like to thank Kelley, our sheepdog, who is a permanent fixture in my office--willing to play, ready to sleep.

Appendix 1, Chapter 5

The CDC System

1. Mission/ Strategy

Unit Mission

Our unit exists to serve our retail customers and consumers

- To effectively sell and service the total beverage portfolio, providing a single point of contact for customer enquiries, and prompts resolution of issues.
- To effectively serve our retail customers, we must also serve our internal customers. We must understand their requirements and deliver excellent service.
- Be must also build shareholder value by controlling costs, improving productivity and continuing to grow professionally.

Business Unit Strategy

To drive profitable volume growth by shifting from a field sales structure to a centralized telephone sales structure:

- Focus on customers and consumers
- Strengthen our competitive position
- Enable sales force to concentrate on outlet development rather than order generation
- Drive efficiency

2. Key Indicators

Functional Indicators:

- Quarterly sales target by tell-sales agent and by channel
- Calls per day-90-100
- Strike rate(ratio of orders to calls)
- Full goods returned due to incorrect order taking/invoicing
- Volume Generating Activities

Customer Satisfaction Indicators:

- Timely resolution of customer enquires
- Retail Customer Satisfaction Surveys- 2 times a year
- Internal Customers Satisfaction Surveys—benchmark annually

Execution Indicators:

- On-Job Coaching—actual Vs monthly plan
- Sit-in and evaluate review meetings with standards checklist

3. Tracking
• Margin Minder software--sales by outlet by agent • Promotions booked, new product intro., etc.–manual tracking posted on display board • CRM software-provides sales history by customer for pre-call planning • CTI software-links call-ins to CRM to deal with enquires
4. Coaching
• Current skills of agents were assessed with skills matrix and plans developed. • Supervisors conduct on-job coaching–3 coaching sessions per agent per qtr. • Coaching-against-a-variance as required. • Regular monitoring of telephone sales calls versus call standards • Sales scripts for new products and promotions.
5. Review
• Daily key indicator results by agent posted on display board. • Weekly team meetings to review weekly targets by agent. • Internal customers (Key Account Mgr, Future Consumption Mgr, Immediate Consumption Mgr, and Distribution Supervisor) attend meeting to monitor service level agreements and to plan coordinated outlet development. • Performance variances caused by a skill-deficiency become part of on-job coaching plan for next week • Performance related bonuses (30% of fixed salary) • CSC manager attends and is reviewed at the monthly sales department review meeting

Appendix 2, Chapter 6: A Case Study

Major breweries in the United States have positioned themselves as high volume, low cost producers with limited plants in strategic locations that rely on wholesaler networks to distribute their products to market.

In the past they have been able to minimize the threat of new, large-scale breweries because of their: dominant share of market, economies of scale, brand recognition, and high advertising spend. There are however a variety of threats and concerns that do exist.

5 Factor Analysis		
Factors	Examples	Threats/Opportunities
Bargaining Power of Suppliers	• Metal cans • Glass containers • Paperboard packaging • Closures • Raw materials	• Consolidation of our major packaging suppliers has limited our ability to leverage one against the other in order to obtain favorable terms. • Raw material suppliers such as fructose are diverting output to other end-use industries, thereby reducing availability and driving prices up. • Maintain at least two financially secure suppliers for each supply category. • Negotiate long term supply agreements (3 to 5 years) to achieve lowest cost and high standards of quality and service.

Bargaining Power of Customers	• Supermarkets • Independent groceries • Convenience stores • Restaurants—nightclubs, bars • State Liquor Stores • Transportation industry • Recreational industries • Internet sales	• Continue to improve the sales and distribution systems to wholesalers to achieve availability ad activation at the point of sale • Continue to build category management partnership with major customers. • Focus on market segments with greatest growth/revenue potential. • Where legal, develop and implement wholesaler promotional support programs. • As needed, implement wholesaler financial support programs to improve cooling capabilities and product quality throughout the distribution cycle
Treat of Substitute Products	• Mild • Tea • Coffee • Juices • Water • Soft drinks • Wine • Liquor	• Add capacity and new technology to supply chain (hot fill, etc.) to satisfy market demand and control costs through the production and packaging cycles. • Use price elasticity modeling with major customers to optimize every-day and promotional pricing. • Continue to bring new products to market that compete with substitutes

Treat of New Entrants	• Financially secure international breweries • Expansion of "house brands" into light or flavor brands • Line extension by other major breweries • Contract packers • New imported beer brands • New micro-breweries • Major domestic breweries • 2nd and 3rd Tier breweries • Mexican breweries • Craft and Micro breweries	• Threat of line extension by major breweries. • Threat of contract packers acquiring their own beverage products. • The strategic issues/options for establishing customers discussed above, also apply to new entrants. • Maintain brand dominance in markets served. • The greatest growth opportunities are outside brewery's core products and markets. • Grow core brands in international markets. • Consider other entertainment thirst quenching opportunities.
Rivalry Among Existing Competitors	• Liquid products: o Soft drinks o Juice o Water o Liquor o Wine	• Direct purchase or partial ownership of foreign companies. • Arms-length ownership of second tier or craft breweries. • Continued differentiation of core products and packaging—new beers including flavored beers and flavored alcoholic beverages. • Improve market execution of the wholesaler/distribution network.

This type of analysis will help you understand the competitive forces that are operating within your business industry. The issues that are generated by the five factors create a broad context for selecting the best strategies.

Appendix 3, Chapter 10

Review Standards Checklist

Team_______________Team Leader____________________Date______________

1 = Very Ineffective	2 = Ineffective	3. Moderate	4 = Effective	5 = Very Effective	Rating

		Rating
1.	**Rules Of The Road** * Were the rules displayed and reviewed at the beginning of the meeting? * Was "time-out" called when a rule was broken? * Was there a debriefing at end of the meeting?	
2.	**Key Indicators** * Did key indicators have targets or standards set for the performance period? * Were functional, customer, and execution indicators reviewed? * Did the key indicators pass the "5 KI Test", discussed to chapter 7	
3.	**Tracking System** * Was accurate data available on actual performance versus target for the review period? * Were charts and graphs used to simplify the data display? * Did the tracking report have historical data to identify trends and aid in problem solving?	
4.	**Leadership** * Did the leader use the appropriate leadership in running the meeting? * Did the leader seek the involvement of others in solving problem (Style 3) * Did people receive appropriate positive recognition for good results? (Style 2) * Did the leader take control when necessary? (Style 1)	
5.	**3 Question Review—Question 1—"How are you doing?"** * Did people receive positive recognition when results were on or above target? * Were high performers given the opportunity to share key learnings with the team?	
6.	**3 Question Review—Question 2 --"If a problem (a negative variance), why?"** * Did the team "jump to solutions" before they had identified the cause of the problem? * Was data effectively analyzed to identify the cause of a variance? * Were fishbone diagrams displayed and used effectively?	

7.	**3 Question Review—Question 3 –"What are you doing about the problem?"** * Did the team avoid analysis-paralysis? * Did the team use the best problem solving method(s): rational, creative, trial-and-error? * Was action taken?--Was it clear <u>who</u> would do <u>what</u> by <u>when</u> to solve the problem?	
8.	**Get Around the Table?** * Did the meeting start and end on time? * Did the meeting leader keep the review on track, controlling digressions? * Were issues that required more information or time "tabled"?	
9.	**On-Job Coaching** * Were coaching plans developed for variances involving a skill-deficiency? * Were coaching plans for the previous performance period reviewed? * Did performance improve as a result of the coaching?	
10.	**Recap** * Did this meeting start with a review of follow-up actions from the last review? * Was a recap kept for this meeting? * Is a copy of the recap distributed to those at the meeting?	
	Total Rating –out of a possible 50 points	

Managers often keep a file of completed checklists to monitor their subordinates' progress in leading review meetings. The most common causes of ineffective review meetings are poor execution of four specific standards - 1, 4, 6 and 7. Meeting leaders often need more coaching in these areas.

Index

Lightning Source UK Ltd.
Milton Keynes UK
13 November 2009

146210UK00001BA/152/P